IS IT SAFE TO DRINK THE WATER?

By Art Buchwald

DON'T FORGET TO WRITE

HOW MUCH IS THAT IN DOLLARS?

IS IT SAFE TO DRINK THE WATER?

IS IT SAFE TO

Art Buchwald

DRINK THE WATER?

ILLUSTRATED BY *Laszlo Matulay*

CLEVELAND AND NEW YORK
THE WORLD PUBLISHING COMPANY

Published by The World Publishing Company
2231 West 110th Street, Cleveland 2, Ohio

Published simultaneously in Canada by
Nelson, Foster & Scott Ltd.

Library of Congress Catalog Card Number: 62-17153

FIRST EDITION

In Place of an Introduction

MR. WILLIAM TARG, EDITOR
THE WORLD PUBLISHING COMPANY
119 WEST 57 STREET
NEW YORK 19, NEW YORK

Dear Bill,

You have asked me if there is anyone I wish to dedicate this book to, as it seems to be the practice of publishers to allot the first blank space in the book to the author to say something nice about his wife, his children, some dear friend, or his mistress who sat up with him all night while he typed the manuscript.

I have given the dedication problem serious thought. I don't wish to dedicate the book to my wife since she's mentioned quite a bit in the book, and just one more word about her and it will go to her head. There is no reason to dedicate this book to my children since they did everything they could to stop me from working on it. I could dedicate it to my father, but if I did he would only go out and buy so many extra copies it would break him.

I don't have a friend I can think of who did much to encourage me in my work. As a matter of fact most of my friends, when I told them I had to work on it, always seemed to reply, "The hell with work, let's play gin rummy."

It is too early in my life to dedicate a work to my mistress,

7

because the way these books sell I can't afford the luxury of having one.

This seems to take care of almost everybody.

When I look back and try to think of some outside credit responsible for this work I can only think of one thing.

So without further ado I wish to dedicate this work

TO MY EXPENSE ACCOUNT WITHOUT WHOSE GENEROSITY, UNDERSTANDING, AND CONSTANT PADDING THIS BOOK COULD NEVER HAVE BEEN WRITTEN.

Sincerely,
Art Buchwald

Contents

CONTENTS

2. IS IT SAFE TO BE IN SHOW BUSINESS?

3. IS IT SAFE TO BE AN AMERICAN?

4. IS IT SAFE TO BE IN POLITICS?

5. IS IT SAFE TO HAVE A FAMILY?

6. IS IT SAFE TO LIVE IN PARIS?

CONTENTS

7. IS IT SAFE TO VISIT THE U.S.A.?

CONTENTS

1.

Is It Safe To Travel
in Europe?

Dinner Guest for Rent

A FEW years ago I wrote about the shortage of guests on the Riviera, and pointed out that while everyone had a villa or a yacht, the natural resources in house guests and boat guests were drying up fast, and unless a guest conservation program was instituted, the people along the Riviera would soon find themselves dining and sailing alone. Well, they scoffed at my warning, but this year the Riviera is facing its worst guest shortage since Elsa Maxwell tried to get a passenger list together for a cruise of the Greek islands.

The profiteering in guests this year is unimaginable.

I know, because that's how I was paying for my vacation. It happened by accident, but if a fellow doesn't take advantage of a situation, he'll wind up spending his own money on the Riviera, and who wants to do that?

It seems that fellow columnist John Crosby showed up in Monte Carlo and innocently asked me if I could get him invited to the Red Cross dinner and gala at which Sammy Davis, Jr., was going to entertain.

I pretended it would be difficult but said I'd do my best. What I knew but John didn't was that the ratio of women to men along the Riviera was six to one, and hostesses were willing to pay anything for a single man to sit at one of their tables.

An hour later I was down at the beach making discreet inquiries. I was tipped off that a Mrs. Max Kettner of New York had three extra women for the gala and was getting desperate.

"How would you like to have Crosby at your table?" I asked her.

"Bing Crosby?" she asked.

"Listen," I said, "if I had Bing Crosby, I wouldn't be here—
I would be negotiating at the Palace with Princess Grace.

"My boy's John Crosby, but he's been a helluva dinner
guest in his time. He's eaten at Bill Paley's house, he's broken
bread with Mrs. Leland Hayward, he's had coffee with Desi
and Lucy twice. This guy is no bum—he's Yale '36, and that
gives him a presold table audience right there."

Mrs. Kettner wet her lips. "How much are you asking for
him?"

"It depends," I said. "Do you want him for cocktails before
the dinner?"

"What's the difference?" Mrs. Kettner wanted to know.

"Well, I can book him for cocktails before the gala at the
Hotel de Paris with another party, and that would cut down
the price for you. He could join you for dinner around ten
o'clock."

"I think I should have him for cocktails," Mrs. Kettner said.
"But I'd better warn you that I don't want to pay more than
$1,500 for the evening."

"Fifteen hundred dollars?" I said. "Why, I turned down
$2,000 from Sam Speigel for Crosby to lunch with him on
his yacht, and Crosby didn't have to put a black tie on either.
If you're going to start talking chicken feed I'd rather have
Crosby stay in his room tonight."

"I'll pay $1,750," Mrs. Kettner said.

"This is ridiculous. I couldn't get you a golf caddy for
$1,750 tonight. Look, Crosby's a syndicated columnist, he's a
name. You pair him up with one of your female guests and
she's going to be impressed—this guy's got class. I'm not going
to sell him out for a song."

"Well, how much do you want?" Mrs. Kettner said.

"The same as Sammy Davis, Jr., is getting for entertaining
tonight," I said.

"But that's outrageous!" Mrs. Kettner replied.

"Look. Entertainers are a dime a dozen," I said. "Where
are you going to find dinner guests at this late date? After

all, Davis will only be on stage entertaining; Crosby will actually be at your table sitting with you."

Mrs. Kettner finally agreed, provided Crosby also would come for cocktails.

I pocketed the money and then rushed back to tell Crosby the news that I had managed to get him invited to the gala. Tears of gratitude poured from his eyes. "How can I ever thank you?" he said.

"Forget it, kid," I said, punching him lightly in the shoulder. "You can do a favor for me sometime."

To this day Crosby doesn't know how much he is worth. He still thinks I did him a good turn. If I only had three Crosbys a season, I could make enough dough to retire for the rest of the year.

The Rabinowitz Plan

THE UNITED STATES is making an effort to attract foreign visitors to its shores to balance the $1.1 billion deficit caused by Americans traveling abroad. Congress recently passed a bill setting up a United States Travel Service to attract foreign visitors to American shores, and for the first time in years Americans as well as foreigners are being told that travel is a two-way street—whatever that means.

I am sorry I wasn't consulted about the United States Travel Service, because I have very strong feelings on the subject, and I even have a plan which would solve all the foreign tourism problems in the United States at no cost to the American taxpayer. I have been trying to present this plan at the American Society of Travel Agents' convention in Cannes, but no one will listen to me, so I decided to take it to the people.

It's called the Rabinowitz Plan, named after my good friend Sam Rabinowitz. He had nothing to do with the plan, but Sam's always complaining no one ever named anything after him and he's getting pretty fed up about it. I don't care who gets the credit for the plan, as long as it's implemented.

To understand the Rabinowitz Plan you have to understand our foreign aid program. For the past several years we have been giving billions of dollars in military aid to different countries to shore up the governments who wish to defend themselves against Communism.

As soon as the military aid arrives, in the form of tanks, guns, and planes, it is turned over to the army, which uses the stuff to take over the governments we have been shoring up. These military *coups d'état* have been very embarrassing to the United States because without American equipment they could never have taken place.

The more military aid poured into a country the more *coups d'état* there are, and, in the end, the American taxpayer has nothing to show for his money except photos of former cabinet ministers being strung up by deadpan army colonels.

Now, the Rabinowitz Plan would take the money we spend on military aid and use it for American tourism.

If the deficit for tourism is $1.1 billion, that money should be distributed to foreigners individually on condition that they use it as tourists to visit the United States. In order that they don't spend it on visiting France, Italy, or Hong Kong instead, we might distribute it as scrip which could only be used in the United States.

If we gave foreigners the opportunity to visit the United States without any cost to themselves, they would probably become much more interested in coming than they are right now, and pretty soon there would be a flood of tourists to the United States making up for the flood of American tourists going abroad.

The foreign tourists would be spending the entire $1.1 billion in the United States, which would wipe out the tourist deficit and balance the flow of gold. It wouldn't cost the American taxpayers anything, because they have already given the money for military aid, which no one sees anyway.

One of the biggest complaints Americans have is that they never see where their tax dollars are going. With the Rabinowitz Plan they will be able to see their dollars actually being spent in America for American things.

The foreign tourist, since he isn't spending his own money, will be less demanding than tourists usually are, and therefore will have warmer feeling for the United States than he would have if American aid were used to knock off his government.

To make it easier for foreign tourists to come to the United States, we would send Polaroid cameras, post cards, plastic luggage, guidebooks, and low-heeled shoes, which would be distributed to them as CARE packages.

Even foreigners with Communist tendencies would be attracted by a free trip to the United States with all expenses paid. We could organize guerilla forces on bus tours and after they have seen Disneyland we could win them over to our side.

The Rabinowitz Plan is foolproof and will do for American tourism what the Marshall Plan did for European industry.

Some day they will build a statue to Rabinowitz for his great contribution to international tourism and understanding. I only hope I can be there at his side when the unveiling takes place.

Invitation to Shoot: I

I was invited to go shooting in England. Shooting is not to be confused with hunting. You shoot birds—you hunt foxes. Of course, you can shoot foxes if they're trying to get at the birds you're shooting, and many people do, but that isn't what the sport is all about.

To be frank, I had no idea what the sport was all about, nor how seriously it is taken in England. People wait all their lives to be invited to shoot birds and still don't get an invitation, while somebody like myself, at thirty-six years of age, gets invited just like that.

I couldn't help being both proud and at the same time apprehensive. Not that I hadn't shot before—winning two poupée dolls and a bottle of white wine at a Pigalle shooting gallery last summer was no mean trick—but I understood live birds were another matter. So counting on the British spirit to take pity on their poor American bumbling cousins, I hied off to Holland and Holland, the gunmakers, to get the drill.

As I entered the shop I saw an Indian maharajah aiming his shotgun in the air at a giant moose on the wall, a Saudi Arabian prince swinging his around the room, and a Guard officer practicing the manual of arms.

"I've been invited to go shooting," I told the man who came up to wait on me, "and I'd like to buy a gun."

"We don't sell guns," he replied. "We fit you for a gun."

"Well, after you fit me for a gun, what do you do with it?" I asked.

"Then we sell it to you."

"Can't you just sell me a gun without a fitting?"

"No, sir. You see, Holland and Holland won't let you have a gun unless we measure you for one. We must take in the length of the neck, the strength of the eye, the breadth of the shoulders, and the depth of the chest, as well as the jowl of the cheek. Your jowls, incidentally, will fit very nicely over the butt of the gun."

"Thank you," I said, warming up to the chap immediately. "Well, if you think a fitting is necessary, go right ahead."

He put a tape measure up to the right jowl.

"By the way," I asked, "how much does a gun cost?"

"Seven hundred and fifty pounds for one, and fifteen hundred pounds for a pair."

The jowl fell. "That's $4,200."

"I believe it is," he said, as he paced off my neck.

"Well, you don't get invited shooting every day," I thought to myself. "Can I have it by Wednesday?" I asked him.

"We are quoting delivery of fourteen months," he said, sizing up the depth of my chest.

"But I'm going shooting on Thursday," I said. "I've got to have it by then."

"I'm sorry, sir. Fourteen months is the soonest we can deliver."

"Couldn't I just buy one off the rack?"

The salesman became slightly pale. "It's been done."

"I won't tell anybody," I begged. "It will be our secret. Just the two of us."

I finally persuaded him to sell me one off the rack for £250 ($700), and as luck would have it, the jowl fit perfectly over the butt. Only an expert, or possibly a pheasant, would know the gun hadn't been made for me.

"What else do I need?" I asked him as he was putting the gun into the case.

"A shooting stick," he said.

"But I'm going to be shooting with the gun."

"You don't shoot with a shooting stick," he said very patiently. "You sit on the shooting stick when you're not shooting. It's a portable seat."

"Do I have to be fitted?" I asked.

"We'd prefer it," he said.

"I can't get one of those off the rack either?"

"It won't take long," he said, putting the tape measure around my hips. "Yes, you need a rather large one, I'm afraid."

The shooting stick cost £15 ($42). Then I was outfitted with cartridges, a cartridge belt, and a flask. After receiving all the packages, I confessed to the salesman that I had never been shooting before.

"I would have never guessed it, sir," he said.

"Would you give me some hints so I won't make a fool of myself?"

"Well, if you don't mind me telling you, I wouldn't wear a red hat when I went shooting," he said, "like you people do in America."

"Don't wear a red hat?" I repeated. "Why not?"

"It's quite insulting to the other guns. If you wear a red hat you're implying that they are such dangerous shots that you have to protect yourself."

"Good point. Now what should I wear?"

"Dress is not as rigid as before the war," he told me. "You can wear plus fours—I think you people call them knickers—long wool socks, ankle-length boots, checked Oxford shirt, and a soft Paisley tie. One doesn't wear a London tie if one can help it."

"What about a hat?"

He hesitated a minute and then said: "The one you're wearing will do perfectly."

Invitation to Shoot: II

THE invitation to shoot came through a friend, Mr. John King, who was shooting at the stately home of Burley on the Hill as the guest of Colonel James Hanberry. Mr. King is the kind of friend who agreed to take me with him knowing full well if I killed any of the other guests by accident, he would never be invited back to Burley on the Hill again.

It's not very expensive to shoot pheasant in England. All you really need is a pair of $4,000 shotguns, plus fours, a loader, a Lapland retriever, a Land Rover, and a gamekeeper.

Mr. King provided most everything for me except plus fours and coat, which I bought secondhand from Moss Bros.

"They belonged to a chap named Chatterley," the salesman explained. "But he never did much shooting in them."

"Why not?" I asked.

He replied: "Unreliable gamekeeper."

The salesman must have been right, because when I arrived at Burley on the Hill one of the other guests admired my plus fours and said: "How extraordinary! Chris Chatterley had a suit just like that!"

There were eight guns shooting that day (a gun is a person,

in sporting language) and Colonel Hanberry had 500 pheasant scattered about his 6,000-acre estate. Each gun was given a place to stand, and then the colonel's beaters were sent out to beat the pheasants toward us. As they flew out, we were expected to knock them down, and when the drive was over our dogs were sent out to retrieve the birds, which were placed next to our peg, indicating how many we bagged.

You're never supposed to brag as to how many pheasant you shoot, because it shows you have a preoccupation with numbers and are not interested in shooting for the sake of shooting itself.

The truth of the matter is, if you have a good, dishonest dog, he can steal everyone else's pheasants and no one will be the wiser. Unfortunately Mr. King gave me an honest dog named Jane, who refused to collect any pheasants except ones that I shot down myself. This, plus the fact that Mr. King's gamekeeper, a man named Moore, who had once loaded guns for King George VI, was standing right beside me, made it very difficult for me to pile up any pheasants next to my peg.

There are about six or seven drives a day when you're pheasant hunting. Once Jane saw how I was shooting she went to sleep. Mr. Moore wasn't as lucky.

By the fourth drive even Mr. King was starting to doubt my shooting ability. But then it happened. A pheasant came flying fifteen feet over me. I aimed carefully and pulled the trigger. "You got him, sir," Moore shouted excitedly. "Right in the head."

The pheasant was still flying, so I felt a little confused. "I did?"

"Yes, sir, right over there. It's a lovely hare and you hit him right behind the ear."

"That's true," I said. "I was afraid he'd get away."

The other guns came over to congratulate me and pat me on the back.

"It was just an accident," I said, trying to hold in my pleasure.

"He's a modest chap," one said to the other. "Not typical for an American."

After that I had no trouble at all. When I wanted to shoot a pheasant I aimed at a hare, and when I wanted to shoot a hare I aimed at a pheasant.

They hadn't seen shooting like it at Burley on the Hill in years.

At the end of the day I had impressed everyone.

Well, almost everyone. The only one wise to me was Jane, who knew exactly what I was doing. But she didn't say anything, probably because she was so grateful to have gotten through the day without being shot herself.

All I could think of as I walked back to the house was how proud Sir Christopher Chatterley would be after his unhappy life to know I had shot pheasant in his plus fours.

Invitation to Shoot: III

MY INTRODUCTION to the country life of England, through an invitation to go pheasant shooting, was most rewarding. If the landed gentry in the British Isles is disappearing, I didn't see it. Everything is the way it was a hundred years ago.

I visited one stately home which was quite large, and to give me some idea of its size I was told a story. It seems the previous week a couple were invited there for lunch.

The roads were icy, there was snow on the ground, and it was about five degrees above zero Fahrenheit. The shivering husband rang the bell and the butler answered the door.

"My goodness, Blagdon," he man said to the butler, "it's cold out today."

The butler bowed and replied: "Wait till you get inside."

It is only natural when you're invited to stay with the landed gentry that you discuss the subjects they're interested in.

Since I had been shooting all day the other guests were quite curious as to how I enjoyed it.

"How did it go, Mr. Buckhurst?" one of the shooters asked me.

"Just fine," I said. "It couldn't be better."

"Do you have pheasant shooting in America, Mr. Billingsworth?" one of the other gentlemen asked.

"I think so," I replied.

My host came over and said, "Mr. Blackman, would you care for some tea?"

One of the men whispered in his ear.

The host looked astonished. "I'm terribly sorry I called you Mr. Blackman, Mr. Billingsworth, but I didn't get your name when you came in."

"It's perfectly all right," I said.

As I was drinking my tea one of the shooters sat down next to me. "I understand you're a journalist, Mr. Goodheart, but you must forgive me, I never read the papers."

"That's all right," I replied, "I write under the name of Buckhurst."

There was a relaxed atmosphere in the room and we got down to serious talk.

"How is Annabelle?" one of the men asked another.

"Not too good. I may have to send her down to London."

"What a pity," someone else said. "Poor Annabelle."

"I didn't know it was that serious."

"Yes, it was a bad fall. I still can't believe it."

"I never thought it would happen to Annabelle," someone said sympathetically.

"Is Annabelle his wife?" I asked the man sitting next to me.

"Don't be a fool. Annabelle is his horse. His wife's name is Julia."

"Where is Julia?"

"She just broke her collarbone and will be up and about in a month. Damned well deserved it, the way she took that last fence. Stephen should have shot her."

"Who, Annabelle?" I asked him.

"No, you clot, Julia."

"Would you and Elizabeth like to come over for lunch next week?" someone asked the man sitting next to me.

"We'd be delighted. Elizabeth hasn't been out for some time."

"Is Elizabeth your wife?" I asked him.

"No, she's my dog," he replied angrily.

"Quite," I said, spilling some tea on my plus fours.

My host came to my rescue. "I suppose this is a different life than the one you're used to, Mr. Bleakhill?" he said to me.

"Oh, no," I assured him. "I always take my dog to lunch."

"Are you married?"

"I was, but I'm not any more. My wife missed a jump in the Bois de Boulogne last week and I had to shoot her."

"Was the horse hurt?"

"Heavens no, or I wouldn't be here today."

American in Rome

THE big mistake was taking my wife to Rome in the first place. Any American husband in his right mind should know better than to bring his spouse to Italy, particularly for the first time. But I underestimated the Italians, which is kind of hard to do.

It all started when my wife came back to the Excelsior Hotel from a shopping trip to the Via Condotti. She had a big grin on her face.

"What's so funny?" I wanted to know.

"Three Italians flirted with me on the street today," she said, pleased with herself.

"Well, don't let it go to your head," I warned her. "They flirt with everybody."

"Don't be too sure," she said. "Besides, the Roman men make you feel like you're really a woman."

"I make you feel like you're a woman, too," I said angrily.

"Did you ever call me Blue Eyes?" she wanted to know.

"No, and for a very simple reason. You don't have blue eyes."

"That's not the point. Even if they lie, they do it beautifully. I think Italian men are wonderful."

I decided to drop the subject before I really lost my temper. But the next day, after another shopping tour, there she stood with the same smile on her face.

"Okay," I said, "what happened today?"

"A traffic policeman stopped all the traffic on the Via Veneto so I could cross the street."

"Big deal," I said. "It so happens that traffic policemen are supposed to stop traffic so people can cross the street. That's their job."

"When the light is green?" she asked. "Then, as I crossed, he tipped his hat and all the cars were blowing their horns. It's never happened to me in any other city."

"Of course, it hasn't. In most cities traffic cops are trying to save people's lives," I said. "So he tipped his hat. He was just looking for an opportunity to take it off. Those helmets can get very hot, you know."

"Don't be so smart," she said. "If you want further proof that Italian men really care, this morning I ordered a coffee at Doney's and the waiter couldn't have been nicer."

"So what? Some waiters are nice. What does that prove?"

"Nothing, except *he* picked up the check."

She was getting impossible and the next afternoon I was afraid to come back to the room.

The smile was waiting for me.

"I know," I said. "You went to Bulgari's and the salesman gave you a diamond necklace as a free souvenir from Rome."

"Nothing that dramatic," she said. "But a taxi driver asked me to go dancing with him tonight."

"Wait a minute. You don't speak Italian. How do you know he asked you to go dancing tonight."

"He held up his hands as if he was holding somebody in them and he hummed a waltz."

"What's so great about that?"

"The cab was moving while he did it."

There was nothing I could say to that, so I tried to walk out of the room.

"I think you're absolutely terrible," she said. "Everyone has been so nice and all you want to do is to throw cold water on me. You American men just don't know how to appreciate a woman."

"Is that so," I said. "Well, it so happens I have a cousin who went up to a girl on Fifth Avenue in New York and told her she had the most beautiful figure he had ever seen, and he's now doing twenty years in Sing Sing. Ever since then I've kept my thoughts to myself."

La Real Dolce Vita

THE FILM *La Dolce Vita* has had a great effect on tourists visiting Rome. It also, I discovered, has had a great effect on Romans. The picture, which graphically describes the decadent life of the modern-day Romans, has forced many of them into roles in real life that they never had any intention of playing.

The other night I was sitting in the Hotel Excelsior bar when I overheard two Italians, presumably man and wife, talking to each other. They were speaking English, because I don't understand Italian.

This is what they were saying:

"Gino," the wife said, "I'm so tired tonight. You sure we gotta go to the orgy?"

"I'm tired too, Carola, but we said we would go, and it's at Claudia's house. You know how mad she gets when she goes to all the trouble of giving an orgy and then the people don't show up."

"But," protested Carola, "her orgies are so dull. She always

makes the pasta with the hashish in it and it's so heavy, I feel
sick for days."

"Is that what she puts in the pasta? I thought it was heroin.
But it's your fault, Carola. I told you the next time Claudia
calls to tell her we already had to go to an orgy somewhere
else. How come you no listen to what I tell you?"

"Because," Carola said, "when Claudia called she said:
'What night are you and Gino free for an orgy?' She don't
ask me to come on a certain night. What could I say? She's
giving it for her cousin's friend from America, because they
gave her a barbecue party when she was in Texas."

Gino said: "Well let me tell you something right now. I'm
fed up going out every night. Why can't we stay home and
read the newspapers and watch the television and maybe
play gin rummy like the other Italian people?"

"Because," said Carola, "we're the *dolce vita* crowd. It's
expected of us. Once the tourist season is over I promise you,
Gino, I make you a nice pizza and we stay home and we
play a game of scrabble."

"And another thing. I'm getting tired of driving around
fast in an Alfa Romeo. I would like a nice small car like a
Fiat."

"You can't drive up to an orgy at somebody's house in a
Fiat," Carola protested. "What will our friends say? You know
how spiteful they are. I don't like an Alfa Romeo any more
than you do."

Carola continued: "Incidentally, Gino, we're going to have
to give an orgy pretty soon ourselves. We owe so many people,
they're starting to talk. I was in the supermarket the other
day and Sophia said: 'How come you and Gino, you always
go to the orgies but you never give one yourself?' "

Gino said: "Okay, but let's do something different instead
of the usual stuff."

"Why don't we give it at the Fountain of Trevi?" Carola
said excitedly. "Then people could throw each other in the
fountain with no clothes on."

"That's been done," Gino said. "The Marquise de l'Acqua

Minerale did it last year. You caught a cold. Don't you
remember?"

"Why don't we show the movies we took last summer in
our palazzo in Venice?" Carola suggested.

"People don't like to look at home movies. It's a big bore.
What about a big costume party; everyone wears a mask and
we give a prize for the best costume."

"It's never been done before," Carola said. "Gino, you're a
genius."

Gino smiled: "You make up the list of people we owe, and
I'll call the caterer tomorrow morning."

"Gino, you think if we ask people to come with clothes on
they'll accept? You know how prudish some of the *dolce vita*
bunch are."

"You give the people free gin and marijuana and they'll always come to a party."

"I guess we gotta go to Claudia's," Carola said. "But let's
leave early. As soon as they start throwing pillow feathers at
each other we go."

Gino said: "Okay, but don't let anyone throw you in the
swimming pool or we'll never get home."

Mau Mau of Rome

IT IS three o'clock in the morning in Rome, and the eerie
sound of tom-toms coming up from the bowels of a Roman
night club can be heard. An American actor staggers out into
the dark, his arm around a deposed princess. Suddenly there
is a shriek followed by the pop-pop of flashbulbs, the murderous click-click of what seems like a thousand camera
shutters going off at once.

The actor cries out in pain, the princess throws her hands
in front of her face, but the firing goes on without mercy.
Finally the pop-pop and the click-click stop, and the attackers

disappear into the dark of the Roman jungle, leaving the actor and princess wild with anger.

The Mau Mau of free-lance photography has struck again.

To the Romans they are known as *papparrazzi;* to celebrities they are known as the "unprintables." These free-lance photographers—there may be thirty or forty of them—stalk their prey for nights, hoping against hope they will find somebody important with somebody else's important wife, or an actress walking down the street in her Maidenform bra, or an actor slugging his leading lady into the Fountain of Trevi.

Each *papparrazzo* takes an oath in a tank of developing fluid that he'll die before letting someone important leave Rome without being embarrassed. The king of *papparrazzi* is a thirty-three-year-old Russian named Ivan Kroscenko, who, dressed in a leather jacket and armed with a souped-up motor scooter parked only a few feet away, is waiting for word that another celebrity is on the loose in Rome.

Neither the police nor libel suits nor the threat of violence can keep Kroscenko from making his appointed rounds.

I had an opportunity to speak to the king during a lull in the *dolce vita,* and I discovered that Kroscenko believes the *papparrazzi* perform a definite function in Roman night life and are constantly being misunderstand by the people they are trying to knock off.

"Everybody likes his picture in the newspaper," Kroscenko said. "Even when it's a delicate situation they like it, though they pretend they don't. They say we're aggressive. Who makes us aggressive? I used to say to people: 'Please let me take your picture.' They always said No! So now I don't ask, because there is no sense in being polite."

The *papparrazzi* live from negative to negative. They sell their pictures to Italian newspapers and magazines for as little as $2 a picture (a roll of film costs almost that).

But they live for the big ones that may get published around the world. Last year Kroscenko, who said he never wastes a picture, caught a photo of Anita Ekberg kicking Frederico Fellini, the director of *La Dolce Vita,* in the pants. This touching shot was published around the world and earned him $200.

He claims to have been the first one to have gotten a shot of Ingrid Bergman and Lars Schmidt together before anyone knew they were going together, and this brought him $600. He lived for weeks on a series of photos of Dawn Addams trying to see her son over the objections of her Italian prince of a husband.

Kroscenko says there is a stock market on celebrities which changes from week to week. Pictures of ex-Queen Soraya bring in hardly anything any more, unless she's with some well-known person late at night. "I got a shot of her with Jacques Bergerac some time ago," Kroscenko said, "and that was good."

He can't get back the cost of his negative for a picture of King Farouk, but he said: "You can do good money with Gina Lollobrigida if you get a picture of her with her child, but not by herself. Sophia Loren alone is now worth good money. I always wanted to get a picture of her in a maternity shot. I could make a lot of money if I got that picture."

"Why? Is she pregnant?"

"No, but everyone would think she was."

Elizabeth Taylor pictures bring in the most money, but then again it depends on where they're taken. Some *papparrazzi* climbed into a villa being built next to the one the Fishers rented in Rome and caught telescopic shots of Miss Taylor in her back yard sun-bathing.

It got wide circulation, proving once again that a picture of Cleopatra in her own back yard is worth a thousand four-letter words—which Mr. Eddie Fisher called the *papparrazzi* when he saw them in the window next door.

The Grave Robbers

I INTERVIEWED a genuine Etruscan grave robber the other day. I shall call him Paolo. He claims he is the chief of all grave robbers in the town of Cerveteri, where the best Etruscan graves can be robbed. Paolo does not shy away from publicity. "Publicity is good," he said, "because then my clients will realize I'm dealing with the genuine merchandise."

A handsome chap in his early twenties, Paolo even offered to give me a photo of himself to make it easier for tourists to find him.

"We grave robbers are victims of unfair business practices," he said. "The black market is full of phony grave robbers selling scandalous imitations of Etruscan masterpieces. Take this little obscene vase here," he said. "It's beautiful, but 80 per cent of the items found in Etruscan tombs are obscene, so the nonobscene items have much more value.

"But the idiot tourists think that because they are obscene they are more valuable. Therefore, the people who make fake Etruscan art specialize in obscene items, so instead of 80 per cent of all Etruscan art being obscene, 120 per cent is obscene, which is entirely too much and gives serious grave robbers a bad name."

Naturally Paolo is violating the law by robbing Etruscan graves, since they belong to the state, but the people of Cerveteri feel anything they find on their land belongs to them. It is this feeling that sent Paolo to jail for eighteen months not long ago.

The trademarks of an Etruscan grave robber are his calluses, and the easiest way to spot a phony grave robber is to ask to see his hands. Cerveteri, Paolo insisted, was the home of authentic Etruscan objects. "The fakes," he said, "are made in the south of Italy, near Taranto.

"In order to get a better price, the imitator may buy an

original piece of art six inches high and copy it two feet high," Paolo went on. "Then he will destroy the original so no one will know about it."

"But isn't that immoral, to destroy the original?" I asked Paolo.

"We would have to agree on the definition of immorality," Paolo said. "If a man, for instance, pretends to be a buyer for a big foreign museum and is in fact a buyer for a big foreign museum, and he can't tell the difference between an original and an imitation, I would say he is an immoral official and the institution that employs him is also immoral. Besides, the Etruscans were pretty immoral, in a sense—you should see some of the stuff we find."

Paolo said he thought the government was wrong in taking what belonged to the people.

"The Etruscans left no will as far as we grave robbers are concerned."

The grave robbers of Cerveteri learn their trade while digging for Italian archaeologists for as little as $1 a day. Once they found out how to discover the Etruscan tombs, they went into business for themselves.

Cerveteri was a great burial place. What makes it one of the busiest places in Italy is that the archaeologists dig in the daytime and the grave robbers dig at night.

"The traffic around here is nerve-wrecking," Paolo said.

"Even the King of Sweden was digging around here. We got into a lot of trouble because of him."

"How's that?"

"He found a tomb and they made a hole and photographed the contents which had marvelous things in it. But the King made a big mistake."

"What did he do?"

"He decided to wait until the next day to actually open the tomb. That is, to find the door and dig the earth out. He went back to Rome to invite his family and government officials to Cerveteri to watch him dig out the tomb."

"What happened?"

"*Someone* opened the tomb during the night and the next morning there was very little left for the King of Sweden. Since then the police have been very mad at all of us and have made life harder. We have had to use all sorts of ruses.

"We used a girl to reconnoiter for a while. One of our men would go out in the field with her after dark and the police would think they were lovers and would be too embarrassed to follow them. It was a good trick, but it didn't last."

"Why not?"

"On one of the scouting trips she got pregnant, and I, as the chief of the band, had to marry her. We have a nice little boy."

The Anatomy of a Gala

ONE of the most ancient of all fertility rites in the tiny Principality of Monaco is the Friday-night gala, a weekly folk festival which is celebrated on the verandah of the Sporting Club of the summer gambling casino. The most gala of all galas is the Red Cross Charity Ball, which also happens to be Prince Rainier's and Princess Grace's favorite gala, and is considered a must for any gal who has anything to do with the rock market.

It is quite possible that one or two of my readers have never been to a Monte Carlo gala, so let me tell you a little about it and you can live on through this story.

The first thing the Casino does is book a big name star to entertain the people. In this case Sammy Davis, Jr., was the draw. The Casino's choice was based not only on the fact that Mr. Davis is one of the best entertainers in the business today, but also because he does not speak any French. If there is anybody the people in Monte Carlo are attracted to, it is somebody who doesn't speak the language. It isn't that the people here dislike anyone who speaks French; it's just that in the summer English happens to be the official language and it would be very insulting to the guests if anyone addressed them in French.

When the people heard that Sammy Davis, Jr., was going to entertain, they automatically assumed that Frank Sinatra, Dean Martin, and Peter Lawford, all of whom were in the vicinity at the time, would also entertain and that they would get four stars for the price of one (the price being $50 per person, not counting wine or Evian water), but at the last minute Mr. Sinatra got mad at Mr. Lawford and flew back to the United States, some said in such a fury that he planned to start working for Richard Nixon.

Anyway, all the wives along the Riviera announced to their husbands that they wanted to go to the Red Cross gala come hell or high water, and the battle for tables was on.

There were only 1,200 dinner places available, so for a week before the gala a long line of desperate husbands knelt in front of the headwaiter, forcing francs, dollars, and pounds into his reluctant hands. Many crawled away disappointed and had to tell their wives why they couldn't go. I heard one man on the beach trying to mollify his bitter wife: "I told him there was $50 in it for him if he would give us a table."

"What did he say?" his wife barked back.

"He said at the moment the only thing he had was a table on the island of Corsica and if it was a foggy night he could not guarantee we'd see anything."

At least 2,500 people were turned away, meaning 1,250 wives haven't been speaking to their husbands since. But for the lucky ones, including the Prince and Princess of Monaco, Gregory Peck, Princess Soraya, Joseph Kennedy, Elsa Maxwell, the Aga Khan, and John Crosby, it was a night to remember.

The women emptied their jewelry vaults for the occasion, they zipped up their most beautiful Paris creations, and fussed with their coiffures until until 9:30, when it was time to leave for the gala. The men in the meantime sulked in their Rolls-Royces and their Bentleys, cursing the whole idea, which took valuable time away from the gambling rooms.

After the Prince and Princess were seated, some wiseacre yelled out, "*Rien ne va plus*" (No more bets), and people started eating caviar, lobsters, stuffed chicken, and ice cream with champagne.

During the courses everyone got up to dance. No one really wanted to dance, but it was the only way the wives could get a look at the other wives, so the husbands just steered them around from one corner of the dance floor to the other, leaving the center of the floor completely empty. (Who are you going to see from there?)

At approximately midnight the show started. It is a known fact that the Monte Carlo gala audiences are the coldest in the world. There's a simple explanation for this. If the husbands show any appreciation for the act, the entertainer is liable to do an encore, and since all the husbands want to do is get to the baccarat and roulette tables as fast as possible, they sit on their hands. Of course their wives applaud enthusiastically, but as they are wearing so many diamond rings on their fingers, it dulls the sound.

Therefore, no matter how good an entertainer is in a Monte Carlo gala, he must realize that if he can hear the applause over the lapping of the waves he's a smash hit. Most entertainers don't understand this and are ready to jump into the sea after the show is over.

Sammy Davis, Jr., by Monte Carlo standards, received one of the greatest receptions of any star who has performed here this year. That is to say, you had to strain to hear the lapping of the sea after he'd completed a number. But I made a terrible social blunder. I shouted and applauded his last number, and my host, who was waiting to play chemin-de-fer, became furious. I happened to be the only male in the entire area applauding, and he said to me angrily: "If I knew you were going to behave this badly at a gala, I wouldn't have invited you."

Well, at this moment it started to rain and I was saved. Sammy Davis, Jr., couldn't do an encore if he wanted to.

As a matter of fact, as the rain came down there was such

an exodus for shelter that the Red Cross had to be called in to revive several people who had been trampled in the crush.

On the Art of Stealing

I ATTENDED a very interesting art exhibition in the south of France held by a gang of art thieves to celebrate the fiftieth anniversary of the stealing of the "Mona Lisa." Because they didn't want any publicity, the exhibition was held in the hideout of Louie the Huile, who specializes in second-story thefts of twentieth-century masters.

Each room of the hideout featured a different period, and under each painting was the title of the picture, the name of the artist, the present owner, and the name of the person, or museum, it was stolen from.

Next to each picture sat a bodyguard with a machine gun.

"We had a hard time," Louie the Huile told me, "getting these guys to loan their important thefts, because the underworld collectors are becoming so frantic about art that they're starting to steal from each other. There are just so many good pictures around, and because of all the publicity about recent art thefts, it's getting more difficult for the guys to complete their collections."

"That's a beautiful Goya over there," I said.

"Yes," said Louie. "It's probably the best 'Duke of Wellington' in existence. It was loaned to us by the Piccadilly Lock Pickers. They never thought they'd get it out of the country. Frankly, I'm not much for eighteenth-century masters, but the English are queer for them, and each to his own taste."

"What's that fellow over there doing?"

"That's Arnaud La Gouache. He pulled the St. Tropez job, but he's still kicking himself because he didn't take the Seurat on the second floor. I keep telling him the Vuillard and the Derain were worth all his trouble, but Arnaud has another

Vuillard from a previous job and he doesn't have Seurat. He
keeps berating himself for being in such a hurry."

We came into a large crowded room devoted to nothing
but Cézannes.

"These belong to Pierre Le Fauve," Louie said. "He just
came back from Aix-en-Provence. Pierre has wonderful taste.
He hasn't stolen a bad picture in the lot."

"That's an interesting picture there, the one of the two men
playing cards," I said.

"Yes, that seems to be everyone's favorite. Maybe it's because all of us play cards at one time or another. Pierre's been
offered four completed Riviera jewel robberies for the picture,
but he refuses to trade.

"I can't really blame him. You can pull a jewel robbery any
time, but there is only one Cézanne 'Card Players.' Most men
would have been satisfied with just that picture, but not
Pierre. He took the lot. We're very proud of him."

"What's in this room?" I said.

For the first time Louie scowled. "Our American friends
from Pittsburgh loaned us these from the stolen Thompson
collection. I apologize, monsieur, if I hurt your feelings, but
the American art thieves are uncultured oafs and don't belong
in the business. Look how they damaged the pictures getting
them out of the frames. And look how badly they're hung.
These men are obviously in it for the money and not the
aesthetic value.

"The only reason we borrowed the paintings is that they
had some early Picassos and some from his cubist period that
none of us in Europe have been able to lay hands on. But I
assure you, monsieur, the art underworld takes a dim view of
the sloppy work the Americans pulled during this job; it gives
art looters everywhere a bad name."

We passed through several other rooms. One was filled with
Egyptian art stolen from the Cairo Museum. "Pepe of Aswan
owns these," Louie said. "He was bored with impressionists
and the modern masters and decided to go off on his own.

There's not much market for this stuff, but Pepe said he collects it for his mummy.'"

In the last room we found a man sitting all alone, tears rolling down his cheeks. The walls were completely blank.

Louie whispered to me: "That's Roger L'Abstract. He made us promise that abstract paintings would be represented, so we set aside this room. He was going to fill it with Jackson Pollocks and he went all the way to Venice to pull the job. But once he got in the house the Pollocks were so big he couldn't get them out the window. It almost broke his heart.'"

Back to Nature

I AM happy to report that in a world that is becoming more American in its living habits, dress, and culture, there is a tiny corner of Europe that still jealously guards its ancient traditions and folklore. Despite the outside world constantly knocking at its door, the people here prefer to live in the past.

I am talking, of course, about Finnish Lapland, the Land of the Midnight Sun, where when a man says "I'm going to take two Lapps around the track," it means he's taking two people to the horse races.

This week I visited the Arctic Circle town of Rovaniemi, which is known as the Paris of northern Finland. Rovaniemi is the gateway to Lapland and it is here that one can study the quaint habits of the people which, while they may seem funny to us, seem perfectly normal to them.

I arrived during the celebration of Midsummer Night, which takes place on a hill overlooking the town. An estimated twenty thousand natives participate in the ceremony and for a stranger it is a thrilling sight.

The first thing that impressed me were the native costumes. The girls wore sweaters and skirts, and the younger ones wore things on their feet called bobbysox. The men were dressed in white shirts, colored ties, and three-button suits. I didn't have the heart to tell them that two-button suits are now in fashion.

The second thing that impressed me was the quaint music which was being played for the native dances. The people in Lapland play special things called records. These records are placed on primitive machines called hi-fi phonographs and the sound blares over the hills. The people's favorite singers, though the names probably mean nothing to most people outside of Lapland, are Elvis Presley, Frank Sinatra, Ella Fitzgerald, and Stan Kenton. To show you how much in the past the people live, the younger children still dance rock 'n' roll, and the older ones who prefer to dance on the Roof Garden at the Hotel Polar prefer the tango.

During the celebrations, at which time the people drink many alcoholic beverages, I had a chance to talk to a few of the natives.

One man asked me if I would like a drink and I playfully asked: "Could I have a Scotch on the rocks?"

"We don't have any," he said, ashamed to appear a bad host, "but could I mix you a whisky sour?"

I met a young lady, attractive in her own way, if you consider someone who looks like Marilyn Monroe attractive, which I understand many Finns do. But for an American visitor it seemed strange to talk to someone who didn't even know that the Marilyn Monroe hairdo was out of style and everyone was now supposed to look like Jackie Kennedy. Primitive, you may say, but you must admire their independence in the wake of such a strong trend.

"Where do you get your clothes? Are they spun for you by your mother or by the villagers?" I asked her.

"No," she said. "Our dresses come from Helsinki, though most of the styles are copied from Paris."

"Oh!"

"But we also copy some American clothes, too."

"Where do you see American clothes outside of an occasional tourist?" I asked politely.

"Some of us subscribe to *Mademoiselle* and others read *Glamour*."

"Ah yes," I said. "But don't you ever use reindeer skins for your clothes?"

"Not really. We find nylon stretch ski pants so much more comfortable."

How charming, I giggled to myself; they still use nylon.

And so it went, these wonderful people living in their own world, asking such naive questions as "What the hell is Kennedy going to do about Berlin?" "How come you let Castro push you around?" and "If England leaves the Seven and joins the Big Six, where does that leave us with our newsprint mills?"—questions that only someone in Lapland would think of asking a stranger.

Yes, I thought to myself as I watched two girls water-skiing on the river the next day, perhaps you people in Lapland have found the true answer to happiness, and we who worship the materialistic modern world are wrong.

Dial Beloved 7777

I was invited up to Finnish Lapland to celebrate an ancient fertility rite known as the Midsummer Night festival. Although this holiday is observed throughout Finland as the most important of the year, when the midnight sun burns all through the night, nowhere is it celebrated with as much fervor as above the Arctic Circle, where the people spend so much of their time in the dark.

The Midsummer Night festival is the time when the Finns light bonfires, make wishes, renew friendships, and communicate with the various alcoholic spirits that abound throughout the land. Since no one knows exactly when the Finns started celebrating the Midsummer Night festival, there's a great deal of folklore connected with it, and many wonderful things can happen to someone on this night if one believes in it.

For example, if you collect nine different flowers from a hillside and put them under your pillow, you will see your beloved's face in a dream. And if you hold a ring up to the sun and look through it at midnight, you will also see your beloved. And if you look in a well on Midsummer Night when the sun is shining just right, you will not see your own reflection but that of your loved one.

There are many other things one can do on Midsummer Night. If a girl walks through a wheat field at midnight with no clothes on, making sure no one sees her, she will find her love, because later on, when bread is made from the wheat, the boy who eats the bread must fall in love with her.

This is the kind of stuff Midsummer Night festivals are made of and why I felt I should attend. Unfortunately I had to leave my wife in Paris, but she is always understanding about these things.

At least she seemed to be the day I left.

The first thing I did when I got to Rovaniemi Airport was to rush to the Hill of the Midsummer Night, where the main celebration takes place, and search for nine different kinds of flowers so I could dream of my loved one.

Then I joined some Finnish friends and started the serious part of the celebration, which consisted of holding a bottle of white alcohol to my lips and tipping it upward toward the sun. The farther I tipped it, the stronger the sun became, and pretty soon I could see it in seven colors. The Finns are the most hospitable of people and after two or three tips they suggested I rest on the grass before continuing the celebration. I found a nice open space and settled down to have a Midsummer Night's dream. But dizzy as I was, I remembered to put the nine different flowers under my head and, sure enough, a few minutes later I saw a vision of my beloved.

Her hair was in curlers and apparently I had just woken her up.

"Hello, beloved," I said.

"Don't 'Hello beloved' me," she said angrily. "Do you know what time it is?"

"It's only midnight," I protested.

"Only midnight, huh? But what else do I have to do except

go to sleep while you go running off to Lapland or some crazy place to look at the sun."

"Now don't get sore," I said. "I looked high and low for nine different kinds of flowers I could put under my head so I could talk to you."

"Why don't you use the telephone like other husbands do?" she said.

"Well, this way is cheaper, and, besides, it's more romantic."

My wife said: "There's nothing romantic about me being in Paris and you being in Rovaniemi at midnight and I'm getting fed up with staying at home while you go barging all over the world."

Before I could answer her, she disappeared.

I woke up and only three hundred yards away I saw a farmer's well. I rushed over to it and looked down. The sun was just right because as I looked into the well, I saw my beloved one.

"We were cut off," I told her.

"I know," she said. "It would have been easier to use the telephone."

"Listen, beloved," I said, "you go back to sleep and have a nice rest, and as soon as my work is done, I'll rush back to Paris to you and the children."

"Big deal." She scowled through the water.

Once again she disappeared and this time I took off my wedding ring and held it up to the sun. Suddenly she appeared in the ring.

"We were cut off again," I told her.

"Why don't you go back to your party and forget about me. I don't know why you called in the first place."

"Just to tell you how much I missed you and how dreary it is being in Lapland without you."

"Tell it to the reindeer. Look, the sun is moving, so I'm going to have to say good-by."

"Good-by, beloved."

As she faded from view, she said: "One more thing. I don't care if you drink the water—just don't eat their bread."

Wet Christmas Club

ONE of the best ways to save money for Christmas in England is to give a certain sum every week to your local pub keeper, who puts it away for you until the end of the year in what is called a mutual loan society, or what Americans would call a wet Christmas club.

You can deposit anything from a half-crown to £5 a week into the "society" and then add two bob a week for what is called a booze fund. Two weeks before Christmas you get your money plus about 4 per cent interest and a credit for booze which you can buy in bottles to take home. During the year, if you get thirsty in the pub, you can borrow from the fund to see you through.

The advantages to the pub keeper are obvious. He gets to see his customers once a week, at least, for the deposit. And he also makes some profit on the booze. The advantages to the customer are even more obvious. It's much more fun to save your money in a pub than it is in a bank or post office, and besides, in England people trust their pub keeper more than they do their post office.

I was invited to go with a friend, Mrs. Fred Tupper, to her pub, The Heroes of Alma, in St. John's Wood, for what is known as "pay-out night." This is the night when all the members of the club receive their year's savings and it's a very gala occasion—indeed, the biggest night of the year for the pub owners next to New Year's Eve. Everyone gets very dressed up and free sandwiches and pickled onions are passed around while the members buy each other drinks and congratulate themselves on how foresighted they were in saving their money for the holiday season.

Although I wasn't a member of the Christmas club, I was accepted as one of them. It was a very touching evening. Mrs. Reilly, the owner, had The Heroes of Alma hanging with

Christmas decorations (she broke her arm doing it, which made it impossible for her to wash the glasses, so her customers did it for her). And there were smiles on all faces.

Mrs. Tupper had put in £1 a week and received £54, though she was fined £2 because she hadn't borrowed from her savings during the year.

"You can't run a loan society," Mrs. Reilly explained, "if people don't borrow from it. My best customers are the ones who borrow the most."

The booze fund came to £5 for Mrs. Tupper.

"This savings is a wonderful thing," said a nice old lady weaving next to me. "It gives you a chance to buy some presents for the kiddies and get things out of hock besides. And there's even some left over to have a bash before New Year's."

A Mrs. Leary ("Just call me Dinah, love") told me pay-out night was her favorite evening of the year. "This is the only night I can afford to drink gin in the middle of the week," she said.

"Gin's your favorite drink, then?" I asked her.

"Yes, love. It lifts your heart and makes you cry over Beethoven. Does it do that to you?"

I said I wasn't sure.

"Maybe you're drinking the wrong gin. It's got to be Booth's gin. None of the other gins makes me cry. I can even get tears out of Chopin with a bottle next to the bed.

"Isn't that right, love?" she asked her husband, who was sitting on a bench.

"That's right," he said. "She always gets a good cry over Chopin with a bottle of Booth's by her bed."

"I cried over Hemingway when I read about him in the paper, didn't I, love?"

"That's right," her husband replied. "Had a good cry over Hemingway you did."

"But what about the Christmas club?" I asked.

"That's just the point," Dianah said. "I couldn't afford Booth's gin if I didn't save my money here with Mrs. Reilly."

"And then you wouldn't be able to cry over Beethoven?"

"Now you've got it, love. That's why I think the club is such a fine thing."

"Helps me save my money, doesn't it, love?" she asked her husband.

"That's right. The club's a fine thing. Helps her save her money," he replied.

At this point a man told me: "We have a fine pub here. I hate to use the word. But you can get intellectual conversation here and talk about music and art and all those kind of things. But the young ones aren't saving their money any more. The reason is they don't come to pubs. They go to coffee houses and dance halls. No chance of saving your money there. Then Christmas comes and where are they? Have to borrow from mum and dad, who have been saving their money all year in the pubs."

"That's right, love," Mrs. Leary said. "They all want washing, the young ones do."

The Heroes of Alma paid out £6,000 that night, of which about £100 was consumed on the premises, most of it going for Booth's gin. But I could see the merit of saving your money in a bar as opposed to saving it in a bank. By saving it in a bar you cut out the middleman. Your barman is your banker and you won't find a friendlier chap on pay-out night anywhere.

"Do you have anything like this in America, love?" Mrs. Leary asked.

"No, love," I replied. "The banks in America are starting to look like bars, and the bars are starting to look like banks, but that's as far as we go."

"Did you hear that, love?" Mrs. Leary said to her husband. "They don't have anything like this in America."

"I heard it. I guess they can't have everything."

Ban the Bomb

I TOOK a train ride out to Wethersfield (England) with a group of Ban the Bomb demonstrators, who intended to cause chaos at the United States Air Force base there. My interest in the demonstration was purely scientific, as I wanted to compare the methods of the British police with those of the French police, whose magnificent truncheon-swinging and rifle-butting I've been observing at firsthand for years. It was a French policeman who first said, as he swung his leadweighted cape at a student's head, "You can't make an omelette if you don't crack any eggs."

The British police, I discovered, are much more careful not to bruise their demonstrators, though a certain amount of bruising is unavoidable when you're throwing demonstrators into the paddy wagon.

The Ban the Bombs demonstration at Wethersfield had a twofold purpose. It was originally divided into the walkers-on and the sitters-down. The walk-on demonstrators had promised to crash into the base and sit on the runways and under the giant SAC planes, preventing them from taking off. The sitters were just required to block the air base by sitting in the road outside the gates.

In both cases the demonstrators hoped to be arrested and were prepared to go to jail to publicize their cause. (If they got on the base they would have been arrested for violating the Official Secrets Act, and could have received anywhere from three to twenty years. Obstructing the road, on the other hand, meant a fine or twenty-one days in jail.)

But because they expected 5,000 demonstrators and only 500 showed up, the leaders of the Wethersfield demonstration gave up their plans to storm the base. Therefore, what the 800 policemen had to deal with at Wethersfield was a sit-down demonstration.

There was a certain formality about the Westersfield demonstration. When the demonstrators gathered at the town of
Wethersfield for the march on the base, which was a mile
away, they were met by two chief inspectors, who told them
to form up in columns of four and they would all march together to the gate, the police on the outside as the guides
and the uniformed inspectors a few feet ahead leading the
parade in very orderly military fashion. The only thing lack-
ing was bagpipers.

As they marched along, I asked one of the inspectors: "Are
you prepared to use tear gas, sir?"

"We haven't used tear gas since the general strike of 1926,"
the inspector replied, offended that I would even ask such
a question.

The demonstrators had slowed up and one inspector said to
the other: "I think we better wait for them, sir, or they'll think
we're not in sympathy with them."

The parade finally arrived at the main gate of the Wethersfield base, where the inspectors halted smartly and turned
around. The demonstrators also halted and one of the leaders said to the inspector: "I take it, sir, you are not going
to let us go any further than this?"

"That is correct," the inspector said politely.

"Then in that case, sir," the leader replied, "we shall sit
down."

The entire disarmament group sat down on the right-hand
side of the very wet road and the police stood above them
all along the way. The road was quite narrow, with a muddy
ditch running next to it, and in order to let traffic in and out
of the base, the police had to keep lifting the demonstrators,
who remained absolutely limp, and throwing them over toward
the side.

In the first hour I stood with one of the inspectors as the
throwing of sitters took place.

"Easy there, Williams," the inspector said as one policeman lifted a demonstrator under the arms and threw him
down again. "Steady, Edwards," he said to another, who

was tossing another sitter over the heads of the other demonstrators. "Don't get too excited."

The policemen, who were cold, welcomed the exercise. Actually, the real danger of injury during a sit-down bomb demonstration doesn't come from the police so much as from a demonstrator being tossed onto the other sitters. The sitters provide a cushion for the demonstrator being tossed who has much less chance of getting hurt than the people he descends on at the end of the policeman's throw.

As time wore on, the inspector stopped cautioning his men, and the police felt they could do more good by throwing the demonstrators into the ditch.

One policeman told me the whole secret of picking up demonstrators to toss them was to find their center of gravity. The accepted method of picking them up was left hand under the feet, right under the arms, and then throw. If you were aiming for the ditch, it was best to toss from a standing position. When loading into the paddy wagon, he explained, it's preferable to use two policemen and toss as you would a sack of coal. (It must be mentioned that Ban the Bomb demonstrations are nonviolent and the demonstrators have orders not to resist the police, as their primary purpose is to get arrested anyway.)

As time went on, the police wagon drove up and several of the sitters were tossed into it.

I asked the inspector why some were arrested and some were not, since they were all obstructing the highway. "How do you choose?"

"The nearest ones to the wagon are usually the most convenient."

About sixty demonstrators were carted off. The rest, sore from the hard, wet road but none the worse for wear, stood up at seven and the protest was over.

I must admit the British police treat their demonstrators much better than the French police do, but in fairness to the French police, French demonstrators can't stand nonviolent demonstrations.

As far as I could see, everyone's head was still intact after the demonstration, which is probably one reason the British can't make a good omelette.

Bourbon Street, London

I WAS walking down St. James's Street, the other day with an Irish friend, Patrick Campbell, when we saw a store window with a big sign in it: VISIT THE BOURBON SHOWBOAT. The store belonged to the United States Trade Center, which apparently was trying to get bourbon sales off the ground in England.

"Do you think they're giving any of the nectar away free?" Mr. Campbell asked.

"It doesn't say anything about free drinks," I said, pressing my nose against the window.

"It would be a terrible thing to pass by and then find out later they were giving out samples," Mr. Campbell said.

"It's hard to believe they would try to promote bourbon in England without letting anyone taste it," I said. "Have you ever had bourbon before?"

"No," Mr. Campbell replied. "But if it's free I know I'll like it."

We entered the building, which was constructed like a Mississippi showboat. A tape machine was playing "Way Down Upon the Swanee River" and, except for two school-children, the place was empty.

But in the back, hidden by a curtain, we found a British public relations man who was tending bar.

He was happy to see us—he was happy to see anybody.

He offered to make us anything you could make with bourbon, and Mr. Campbell let it be known that anything the man could make he could drink.

The public relations man said that up until two weeks ago

he had never tasted a drop of bourbon. But now he found it one of the finest drinks he had ever had.

"When did you get the bourbon account?" I asked him.

"Two weeks ago," he replied.

While he was mixing he told us the sad story of exporting bourbon. "The Americans just never tried to export it," he said. "First you had Prohibition, then the war came, and after the war you worried about your domestic markets. Now you're starting to look for people to drink it abroad. But it's rather expensive and for the moment we're going to have to appeal to the upper classes."

Mr. Campbell nudged me and whispered: "Don't ask him so many questions or he'll never get the drinks made."

"I wasn't asking him any questions," I said.

"The trouble with you Americans when it comes to exporting," the man continued, "is that you have never made any attempt to establish snob appeal for American goods. You haven't had to go after foreign markets with what we should call, if you'll excuse the expression, 'hard sell.'"

"Isn't it a little late to get the British to drink bourbon?" I asked.

"Yes and no. You do have people with fixed drinking habits over here, but you also have a floating drinking population who may have gin one time, cognac another or Scotch. They become bored and are always searching for something new."

"If I don't get a drink soon," Mr. Campbell said, "I'm switching back to gin."

"You get a bigger kick from bourbon than you do from Scotch," the PR man said. "As a matter of fact, of all the people I forced bourbon down the throats of, 60 per cent said they liked it."

Mr. Campbell's hands were trembling.

Finally the PR man poured us a drink.

Mr. Campbell tasted it and I waited for his reaction.

"It's delicious," he said. "Absolutely delicious. I don't see how Scotch has a chance, once the British taste this."

The PR man smiled and poured him another, and Patrick was ecstatic. Then a third and then a fourth. After the fifth I told Mr. Campbell it was time to go. He promised the PR man he would return in the evening and bring his friends. We both had one for the road and then we were back out on the street again.

"Did you really like it?" I asked him.

"God-awful stuff," he said. "What the devil do you think they put in it?"

Trouble Spots, Inc.

I WAS talking the other day with a travel agent named Herb Sargent, who was very depressed.

"Every time I try to sell somebody on a trip somewhere trouble breaks out and I get a cancellation," he said.

"We travel agents are victims of tomorrow morning's headlines. I do not know what to do."

"Why don't you organize tours to the trouble spots?" I suggested. "If you made them sound glamorous enough I'm sure people would go."

"You may have an idea there," he said, starting to sketch a poster. "How does this sound: 'Visit South Vietnam and have your picture taken with a real Viet Cong guerrilla'?"

"That's pretty good. Why not group tours? If you get more than ninety people you can hijack your own plane and have a ten-day holiday in Cuba."

"We could sell university tours to South America, where U.S. students could meet South American students and participate in riots with them," he said. "We could arrange with U.S. Information Centers for special tours of the buildings, where they could break USIA windows together.

"How about this slogan: 'Be the first one on your block to be arrested as a spy in East Berlin'?"

"It will sell," I assured him.

"And Algeria. Just think of what we could do there. 'Visit riot-torn Algeria. Stay as long as you like, or, for a special rate, leave on the last plane out.' "

"Don't forget the Congo," I told him.

" 'Gala massacres under the stars. Participate in a thrilling evacuation.' "

"I'm ready to go right now."

"Do you think people want to visit Syria?" he asked.

"It depends if the Israelis attack it again."

"But suppose by the time my tour gets there hostilities have ceased?"

"Then they either get a refund or a chance to visit no man's land along the Gaza Strip."

"There'll be a surcharge if they want to drive over any land mines," Sargent warned.

"Of course, you will lose a lot of guides on a tour like that."

Mr. Sargent said he could arrange with one of the air lines to have special planes fly through the German air corridors, with Russian fighter escorts.

"What about a cruise to the romantic islands of Quemoy and Matsu?" I suggested.

"Or a sail toward the sunset during a nuclear test in the Marshall Islands?" he said.

"Perhaps a palace revolution in Nepal?"

" 'An army uprising in Korea with all tips included,' " Sargent said, making another poster.

"There is no end to the possibilities," I assured him. "People would even pay to be in a hurricane in the Caribbean."

"Or an avalanche in Switzerland."

Sargent didn't know how to thank me enough. "I will call my tours World Trouble Spots, Inc., and our slogan shall be 'Pay Now, Pray Later.' "

The Dream Salesmen

I took a ride down to Cannes to attend the thirty-first convention of the American Society of Travel Agents, known as ASTA. Not everyone who shows up at a travel agents' convention is a travel agent.

As a matter of fact, of the 2,200 people in attendance, only 50 per cent are travel agents—the rest are made up of people promoting travel agents, such as air lines, shipping companies, hotel owners, drive-it-yourself dealers, government tourist officials, and anyone who has the least interest in the difficult, occasionally lucrative, fairly unpredictable business of tourism.

The business of being a travel agent, I discovered, after hanging around with several for a few days, is quite complex. As a travel agent you are selling something that really only exists in the imagination of the customer. Some travel agents claim they sell dreams. Others, like Mr. Louis Bromley, of Cambridge, Massachusetts, sells memories. "My slogan is," he said, " 'Memories are your best investment—you can take them with you.' If you can get that slogan in your story, I'd appreciate it, because my brother is against us using it, and I think it's pretty good."

But, unlike a suit, an appliance, an automobile, the travel salesman has nothing to show the customer except some folders, a few posters, and some very complicated timetables. From these few items he has to talk his customer into making a $1,500 or $2,000 investment. And, unlike a car, a previous trip has no trade-in allowance.

Mr. Bromley said that 80 per cent of all pleasure travel is initiated by women, generally after they have had conversations with other women who have already been abroad. (The other 20 per cent are initiated by the husbands who want to know how they can go without their wives.) The women usually come in first to make inquiries, but, Mr.

Bromley says, less than half of them wind up buying a trip.

"Of course," Mr. Bromley said, " a customer is usually three-quarters sold before she comes into the place, so we only have to sell her the other quarter of the way. Then, after we sell her, she has to go home and sell her husband; but if she's determined to go, there is not much the husband can do."

"What does the woman ask for when she comes in for the first time?"

"She wants to have a trip such as her friend Mrs. Jones took, only better. If Mrs. Jones stayed at the Savoy in London, she wants to know if there is a better hotel she can stay at so she can let Mrs. Jones have it right between the eyes when she gets back home.

"At the same time, anyone who has been abroad once is automatically an expert in travel, and one of the problems a travel agent faces after he has made all the reservations is to get a call from the client who says: 'My friend Mrs. Rabinowitz says the only hotel to stay at in Madrid is the Ritz; why did you book us at the Palace?' "

Mr. Bromley said that men make better travel agents than women and men with slightly foreign accents make better salesmen than anybody. A home run in the travel business is to sell two first-class tickets around the world.

Mr. Bromley said that a wise travel agent never contacts his client until she has been home for two or three weeks. "If you talk to her as soon as she gets home you're liable to get an earful. But if you wait a few weeks, until after she has everything in perspective, she'll usually tell you she had a good time."

Travel agents are constantly thinking up new types of tours to attract business. There are gastronomic tours, wine-drinking tours, theater tours, art tours, jazz tours. A big business now is bachelor tours.

"I know one fellow," Mr. Bromley said, trying to illustrate what a crazy business he was in, "who was running a bachelor tour. It was quite expensive and he was just doing fair at it. But one summer one of the girls on the bachelor tour got pregnant, and the girl's mother sued the travel agent for negligence, though he wasn't even on the trip. We thought the agent was finished, but instead, when the story broke in the newspapers, his business zoomed, and he doubled his bookings overnight."

Come Fly With Me

THE care and feeding of travel agents at a travel agent convention is a thing of beauty to see. All forms of tourist companies, from jet air lines to camel caravans, are trying to woo the travel agent, who is believed to have a great deal of power over his clients as to how and where they will travel and stay. For this reason every suite in Cannes, where the American Society of Travel Agents is holding its thirty-first convention, has been turned into a bar, and the hotel lobbies have been turned into swimming pools of travel folders, and a man has to be fast on his feet or he will never see his wife and children again. For example, I was on my way to the convention hall from the Carlton Hotel when an Indian stopped me and said: "You have never been to India? I am from the government tourist office and we would like you to come."

"That's very nice," I said. "When?"

"Tomorrow."

"Isn't that a little short notice?" I said.

"It will take only a month, unless, of course, you would like to go to Nepal and Ceylon. Everything has been arranged. You will like it very much. I will have you met at the plane in New Delhi. Good-by."

I wandered away, wondering what I would tell my wife, when a man from the Irish tourist office approached me and gave me a cup of Irish coffee. "I saw you talking to the Indian tourist people. They want you to go to India, don't they?"

"I'm afraid so," I said.

"Why don't you stop off in Ireland afterward?"

"Is Ireland near India?"

"It's only a hop and a skip and a jump away. We'll look forward to seeing you there."

Before I could protest he had disappeared. I started to walk down the street when an Arab came up to me and I became wary. "I don't want to go to Egypt," I said.

"Who's talking about Egypt?" the Arab replied. "Come to Syria. It's free." He pressed an air-line ticket into my hand.

Immediately the Israeli tourist representative, who was following the Syrian official around, came up and took the ticket out of my hand. "First Israel, then Syria," he said. "What's the matter, are you anti-Zionist?"

As I was talking, the delegation from the Hawaiian visitors' bureau surrounded me, swinging weighted leis like bicycle chains. "We hear you're going to Ireland and not even stopping off in Hawaii on the way."

"But Hawaii seems so far away from Ireland."

One of the Hawaiians lifted his carnations threateningly and I promised I would drop over to Hawaii from Ireland.

"Don't let those Hawaiians scare you," a man from the Puerto Rico Hotel Association told me as I stood there shaking. "They're not going to like it in Puerto Rico if you go to Hawaii and don't stop off in the Caribbean."

"But," I protested, "I've got to go to India, then Ireland, then Israel, then Syria, and then Hawaii. If I go to Puerto Rico, when will I ever get home?"

"Late next year," a bystanding Japanese tourist official said, giving me a travel voucher, "as long as you don't care about seeing the cherry blossoms. How do you like your bath?"

I tried to push through the crowd, but the Yugoslav tourist official wouldn't let me pass. "If you go to Japan you must come to Yugoslavia. Japanese girls very little, Yugoslav girls very tall. You see the best of both worlds."

"But my wife—" I cried.

Some cowboys from Las Vegas started stoning me with

silver dollars. "Come on to Las Vegas, boy, and we'll show you a time."

"And don't forget the Seattle World's Fair," someone else cried.

Suddenly a voice shouted: "Hey, I've seen that fellow around somewhere. He isn't a travel agent. He's some sort of a newspaper nut."

"How do you like that? He was posing as a travel agent."

I gave the Las Vegas cowboys back their silver dollars.

Each government tourist official came up to me and took his air-line ticket back angrily. Maybe it was just as well. My wife gets kind of mad if I stay away from home more than two years at a time.

2.

Is It Safe To Be in
Show Business?

How I Lost $50,000 in My Spare Time

It was September, 1955, and I was bumming around the Riviera looking for likely subjects for my column. On an off chance I took a ride over to Monaco to look up an old friend, Father Francis Tucker, an American priest stationed in the Principality as rector of St. Charles Church and also confessor and confidant to Prince Rainier III.

Father Tucker, a spry, cheerful man of sixty, invited me to dinner and soon we started discussing Monaco's most pressing problem—which was how to get a male heir for the kingdom. It seemed that if Prince Rainier were killed or died and there were no heir to the throne, Monaco by treaty would revert to France and its tax-free, draft-free citizens would no longer find themselves living in paradise.

Since Prince Rainier was not even married, and since he enjoyed skin diving, big-game hunting, fast car driving, and the lot, the Principality was in peril every day and everyone in Monaco shuddered every time they saw a newspaper photo of their ruler in some dangerous pursuit.

Father Tucker discussed the possibilities of getting the Prince married, and they looked pretty gloomy. It appeared the Prince didn't care for any of the likely royalty prospects in Europe, and except for a short fling with a French actress named Gisèle Pascal, there was no one on the horizon to produce the desired heir.

The priest did mention that Prince Rainier liked the American actress Grace Kelly very much, but at the time so did everybody else.

They had met only once when Miss Kelly had posed for

some publicity photos at the Prince's Palace for the French magazine *Paris-Match* (they walked together through the Prince's zoo) but Father Tucker told me that he and the Prince planned to visit Philadelphia in the near future and perhaps at that time the Prince and Miss Kelly might meet again, and then—well, the priest said, one never knew.

I wrote a column about my conversation with Father Tucker which was titled, "If Grace Kelly Only Cared." I described the situation in Monaco and quoted the priest, with his permission, as to all the ramifications that the lack of an heir was causing. I treated the Prince's crush on Miss Kelly with tongue in cheek, as it was inconceivable to me that a movie star, at the height of her career, would be interested in a Prince whom she had met only once.

A week later a Hollywood producer named Charles Feldman met me in Paris and said he had enjoyed the column very much. He also said he saw a wonderful movie in the situation as I described it. He asked me if I would consider writing a film based on someone like Prince Rainier ("No one knows Rainier," Mr. Feldman told me. "We'll make the guy Aly Khan."). And I agreed.

Since I had never written a movie before, Mr. Feldman introduced me to a writer named Cy Howard, who immediately demanded that Mr. Feldman pay us $100,000 for the script—$50,000 for the delivered script and $50,000 the first day of shooting. Much to my surprise, Mr. Feldman agreed to the terms and the deal was made.

Cy and I worked out a story line. It was decided to lay the story in the Principality and use as a background a film festival. The Prince was everything Aly Khan and Prince Rainier ever dreamed of being. Our heroine, whom we called Lily, was a young American actress whose film was being shown at the festival. We kept the priest in the story because we needed him for matchmaking purposes. We also introduced the Prince's masseur, who was in charge of introducing the Prince to new, beautiful girls. The masseur of course represented the devil. Lily had an ambitious mother and a more ambitious agent, and pretty soon Cy and I were turning out hysterical scene after hysterical scene with great laughs on every page.

My favorite scene had an Anna Magnani-type actress going up to the reception desk at the hotel and saying, "I want a room—without a bath!"

For the next two months Cy and I worked and fought and sweated in typical collaboration form. During pauses in work we discussed what we were going to do with the $50,000 each we were going to get from Mr. Feldman for writing the script. Since Father Tucker gave me the column, Cy suggested I give him the $50,000 to build a new parochial school. But my wife, who is more practical than Mr. Howard, talked me out of it.

Anyway, the first draft was developing into one of the most brilliant comedies ever written for the screen. I had Cy's word for this, and he had mine.

There didn't seem to be any rush about the story since Mr. Feldman was casting around for an unknown to play Lily. Cy and I knew this because every once in a while we bumped into him on the street with a lovely young girl and he'd say, "Boys, wouldn't she make a wonderful Lily?"

This would be our cue to say, "She's perfect." And then Feldman would dismiss us and walk up the Champs Elysées arm with the excited girl gushing beside him.

As far as the Prince was concerned, we discussed Cary Grant, William Holden, Gregory Peck, and Jack Lemmon.

It was obvious to all of us that when Billy Wilder read the script he would insist on directing it.

In the meantime I read somewhere that Prince Rainier had gone to America with Father Tucker but I didn't give it any thought. Who needed them any more?

Then one day one of the fellows in the editorial offices of the Paris edition of the *New York Herald Tribune*, who knew I was working on the script, said I better look at the Associated Press ticker. I walked over to the machine to see the frightening word BULLETIN on the teleprinter.

This was followed by: "PHILADELPHIA—Mrs. John Kelly announced the engagement of her daughter Grace Kelly to Prince Rainier III, ruling monarch of the Principality of Monaco."

I checked the United Press ticker to make sure there was no mistake. UP was also putting out the bulletin. My $50,000 was going up in smoke on both the AP and UP machines.

Numbed, I went back to my desk and put in a call to Cy, who was working on a scene where the priest is telling the Prince unless he straightens out and flies right, the priest is going to resign.

"Cy," I said trying to control my voice, "Grace Kelly is going to marry Rainier."

"She can't!" he screamed.

"Why not?"

"Because we'll sue her. It's our story."

But we didn't sue. Instead I went back to Monaco in April to cover the wedding. Cy went back to Hollywood to work for television. Mr. Feldman broke the sad news to all the Lilys, and in no time at all Monaco had a male heir.

How was I to know that Grace Kelly really cared?

Talk With the Author

RICHARD CONDON, the author of *The Oldest Confession, The Manchurian Candidate,* and *Some Angry Angel,* claims to have written the cowboy novel to end all cowboy novels. It's titled *A Talent For Loving,* and Condon, who is now in Paris, claims that although it is only 291 pages long, it has seventeen more characters in it than *Gone With the Wind.*

Condon says his novel has 8,878 characters in it, including 64 people with speaking roles, 154 with minor roles, including 18 renegades and 1 Papal Nuncio, 1,427 wedding guests, 1 frontier dentist, 2 working clergy, 701 bandits, 1 ruined husband, 16 murderers, 2,203 gamblers, 1,419 cowboys, 1 ruined wife, 514 Indians, not counting 302 ancient Aztecs who appear in a flashback, 8 governors of Mexican states, 32 dance hall girls, 159 conquistadores, 5 acrobats, 4 Scotch shepherds, 2,003 townspeople in three towns, 43 train passengers, and 4 pretty girls.

The author claims he has many firsts in his book. "It is the only novel in the history of the Western novel in which the Indians save the white settlers from an attack by the cavalry," he told me.

"It is the first Western novel which differs from others in an approach to the sociological norm. I decided to correct some serious misconceptions about cowboys in saloons. All Western novels show gunfights in large saloons which are complete with three bartenders and a huge stock of spirits. The only trouble is everyone in the saloon, except for the town drunk, is usually sober. In my book all the cowboys, including the gunfighters, are sloshed to the ears when the shooting starts."

Another first, Condon says, is that in his novel the two cowboy heroes can neither read nor write. "I wrote it this way so that if the book is sold to the movies there will be no top actor we can't get.

"The most popular and best-selling Western novels," Condon told me, "are the family-type saga Westerns that run three or four generations. The United States is only seven generations old, but my family-type saga takes in seventeen generations, all in North America, starting with Cortez. Therefore, I have ten more generations in my book than the United States itself.

"My gunfights have a reality to them that most Western novels lack. I have a legendary Mexican gunfighter who does not notch on his gun butt the white folks he has killed. He only counts Indians and other Mexicans.

"Not all gunfights come off as planned, despite what you read or see in the movies. In one of my gunfights both gunmen have just eaten a suckling pig. Then they draw to have it out, but their hands are so slippery the guns slip out of them, and they have to slug it out instead."

The main part of the book concerns a horse race from the Rio Grande to Mexico City, the winner to get the hand of the beautiful girl. Condon said his novel covers 482,115 square miles of Texas and Mexico. "Writing it," he said, "took me from April, 1959, to August, 1960, so I was actually writing at 1.86 miles per minute."

But before starting his novel Condon did a great deal of research, some of it of great value. For example, he discovered that of the 436 dance hall girls in Texas between 1844 and 1871, only 2 had hearts of gold, only 6 were under forty-three years of age, and their average weight was 153 pounds.

Condon hopes to sell his book to the Viennese Opera company, but failing this he will try to sell it as a children's record. "There's a lot of money to be made from children's records these days," he told me. "And kids have the money to spend."

How To Succeed in Paris

THE biggest Broadway hit since *My Fair Lady* is a show called *How To Succeed in Business Without Really Trying*. It is a musical, and the story concerns a young man, played by Robert Morse, who buys a book on how to succed in business and, by following it, rises from a window washer to the chairman of the board of a large corporation.

Before I left New York, Abe Burrows, who wrote the book and directed the show, asked if I would come over to see him. He said he wanted to discuss with me the possibilities of putting on a production in France.

Mr. Burrows is an old friend, and therefore I tried to dissuade him from doing it.

"Your story is all wrong," I explained to him. "First of all, window washing in France is a very respected profession, and a window washer would rather remain a window washer than become the head of a large company."

"But why?" Mr. Burrows asked.

"Because it takes years of study to wash French windows. Unlike American windows, they're very complicated to clean, and once a man has learned to wash them well he feels he is making more of a contribution to society than he would be doing as a company executive."

"But let's say, for argument's sake," Mr. Burrows said, "that we find one window washer in France who is unhappy in his work. Suppose he gets chills and doesn't like working outdoors. What would be wrong with that?"

"Nothing except that you don't understand the corporate structure in France. Even if you wanted to rise in a French company, it would be very difficult.

"First of all, most corporations in France are still family businesses.

"The chairman of the board is an eighty-seven-year-old man who took over two years ago from his father. His son is sixty-five years old and is still being trained in one of the various departments so he'll learn the business. And his grandson is thirty-seven years old, so he's considered too young to have any responsibility and is only allowed to work in the summertime.

"Therefore, how could a complete stranger, such as your hero, ever hope to rise in such an organization?"

"I got it," said Mr. Burrows. "Suppose my hero, while washing windows, discovers where the second set of books, which all French companies keep, are hidden? Wouldn't that be reason enough to get a promotion?"

"It's a possibility," I admitted. "But you've got to remember one thing. In your show the window washer is so ambitious he keeps ignoring the girl who is in love with him. In fact he ignores all the girls in the show. The French would never believe this. As a matter of fact the only reason a French window washer might want to become the chairman of the board is so he could get his hands on the chairman's secretary. Once he succeeds there, he would probably go back to window washing.

"You see, in France the Frenchman is only interested in getting ahead if getting ahead means getting the girl. Your show violates a basic French principle since your hero wants to get ahead for the sake of success."

"Suppose," said Mr. Burrows, "the window washer is actually the illegitimate son of the chairman of the board. Would that work?"

"Now you're talking," I said. "That happens all the time. Most Frenchmen don't remember, so they usually assume it's true."

"Then the show would work, wouldn't it? My window washer would be promoted over everyone else, wouldn't he?"

"Even over his legitimate son," I agreed. "A French father always favors a son born out of wedlock, as he regards him as some sort of trophy."

Mr. Burrows was joyous. "All I have to do is make a few minor changes. The window washer has chills and therefore prefers to work inside. He also wants to get his hands on the chairman of the board's secretary, but the only way he can do *that* is get the chairman's job, and he does this by proving he is the boss's illegitimate son."

"You make those changes and you can't lose," I assured him. "I can see Maurice Chevalier playing the window washer right now."

In Defense of Beards

ACCORDING to the latest information from the men in the know in the United States, beards are back. This despite the fact that Castro's beard symbolizes everything the American people don't like about beards—too long, untrimmed, curly edges, etc.

I was fortunate enough to talk to Peter Ustinov, a man who has had a beard since 1956 and defends beards without being defensive about it.

"Do you find a beard helps you in your everyday life?" I asked him.

"People seem to respect you more," he said. "They tend to ask for advice and consolation and they think you can solve their problems. Occasionally I've used it to throw rank around. Once I parked in front of the Hungarian Embassy on the Rue de Berri. The concierge of the embassy came running out and said no one could park in front of the embassy. I touched my beard and replied to him in Russian. He went white and dashed back into the embassy again."

Mr. Ustinov said he believes people have a deep-seated human respect for beards which must come from some prehistoric time.

"I noticed when the Peking Opera came to London the wise man in the opera always touched his beard and lifted it with difficulty as though he was weighing his own wisdom. As the Chinese are a very old civilization, I imagine this is a very old gesture."

He continued: "But there are disadvantages to a beard. I will say that. I thought it was a labor-saving device, but now I spend more time explaining why I have a beard than it would have taken me to shave. On a bad day I could shave in fifteen minutes, but it takes twenty-five minutes to explain why I didn't.

"At the same time, women find a beard irresistible and they all ask if they can touch it. They think it brings them luck. Strangely enough, while they may be attracted to someone with a beard, they don't want their husbands to grow one. Many wives think it's too much of an adventure to embark on. They like the idea but they're not prepared to take the risks involved."

"Such as?"

"Well, a lot of men, as soon as they grow a beard, become very aggressive about it, as if to say 'I've got a beard, what are you going to do about it?' Then there are economic taboos about beards. Many employers wouldn't trust a man with a beard. Or if an employer did, customers might not. No, you've got to think twice about a beard."

"What has been the reaction at home about your beard?"

"Rather good," he said. "The first time I had it I paid a visit to my great-uncle, who was eighty-nine years old, and he took one look at me and, with tears in his eyes, said: 'You look like my brother Louie,' who happened to be my deceased grandfather."

"Did your mother like the beard?"

"Why shouldn't she, if I looked like her father?" Mr. Ustinov replied.

"Why do you think the beard is getting popular in America?"

"Americans are always attempting to run away from conformity, but unfortunately they always start running in the same direction."

Mr. Ustinov warned that if someone wanted to grow a beard he should be aware that beards dry quite slowly after you wash your face in the morning. "Occasionally you find yourself in the embarrassing position of being at a large luncheon and one drop of water conserved from the morning tub will suddenly fall on the tablecloth. In winter, when the weather is moist, that drop might not fall until you're at tea.

"Also, a man who eats carelessly should not grow a beard, as he might find himself pursued by pigeons aching to get at that fragment of food which the pigeons can see but the man can't."

Mr. Ustinov said that a man with a beard can also be subject to mistaken identity. He said he was in Rome when a woman came up to him and said: "I won my bet. I knew you'd forget me but I didn't think you'd be unfair as well."

" 'What are you talking about?' I asked her.

" 'You haven't really forgotten? Did that summer mean nothing to you at all?'

" 'I swear I don't know what you are talking about,' I shouted.

"She started crying so hard I had to walk away fast. Apparently all she remembered of the summer was her friend's beard."

Chester Grin in Berlin

IN SEARCHING for new locations for television variety shows, it was obvious someone had to think of West Berlin sooner or later, and somebody did. Jack Paar's producers say they thought of it first, but Ed Sullivan says it was his idea all along. It doesn't really matter whose idea it was. Paar got there first and now the question all Americans must face is not "Will America fight for Berlin?" but "Will America fight for Jack Paar?"

The introduction of Paar into the Berlin crisis was so unexpected even the Russians were unprepared for it. But one American public relations colonel was given the boot and another colonel was given a public tongue-lashing. It could have been worse.

Suppose the Chester Grin Show had taken place from the same spot.

"Good evening, folks. This is Chester Grin, your favorite night owl and sometime disk jockey, reporting to you from the heart of West Berlin where East refuses to meet West, and the twains don't run any more. Ha-ha-ha! Well, we have a lot of laughs tonight and a lot of wonderful acts, but first let's pause a minute for a few cheery words from announcer Hugh Knowit about tooth decay. . . .

"Thanks a lot, Hugh, now back to West Berlin. Tonight I want you to meet some really talented kids, and I mean talented kids. Fellows, look over at the camera. Harry, would you point the camera over here? Thanks, Harry, that's swell.

You boys operate that tank over there, is that it? Would you show our television audience how it works? That's right, get in the tank. They're wonderful kids, aren't they Harry, would you point the camera at the tank? What is that thing pointing out of the turret, boys? Oh, that's a 106 recoilless rifle. Well, what you know about that?

"Why don't you point it at the East Germans, boys? Harry, get a shot of the boys pointing the cannon at the East Germans. How about that, folks? Those talented kids are pointing their cannon directly at the East Germans. I'll bet that gives the Commies something to think about. Harry, what's that tank over there doing? Well, why is it pointing at us? I only asked for one American tank. What's that you say, it's an East German tank? Well, how about that, folks; there's an East German tank pointing its cannon directly at us. This will give you some idea of how tense things are in this city.

"Hold it a minute. While we were talking a couple jumped out of an East Berlin apartment window into a West Berlin street. Maybe we can get them to talk to us. But first we'd better have a word about a new, and I mean new, shaving cream. . . .

"Here we are back in West Berlin and I'm talking to two young East Berliners who have just escaped by climbing down a rope made of sheets. Folks, I know this is a lot to ask of you, but would you re-enact your escape again for our cameras? I mean would you just mind climbing up the sheets again? I think our viewing audience would be interested in how you did it. . . . They don't seem to understand. Would somebody translate for me? I'd like them to re-enact their escape for our audience. Tell them sixty million Americans are watching them. . . . They still don't want to do it? Well, forget it then. It's hard for these people to imagine what appearing on my television show means for someone. I wonder where Bob Hope, Jack Benny, Danny Kaye, or Frank Sinatra would be today if they hadn't appeared on the Chester Grin Hour.

"How many more minutes do we have, Harry? Okay. Let's have a song by—you guessed it—Irving Berlin.

". . . That was swell. Well, folks, it's getting late here on the Friedrichstrasse. The Americans are bringing up more tanks. The East Germans are laying out their barbed wire for the night and we hope you've had as much fun being with us as we have had being here. Good night all!"

The Rocks of Niven

I SAW David Niven in Monte Carlo at a private showing of *The Guns of Navarone* for the prince and princess of you-know-what. He had a faraway look in his eye, and suddenly, without reason, he said to me: "They're probably on my rocks at this very moment."

"Who are on your rocks at this very moment?" I asked him nervously.

"They are—the people. They're my rocks. But they won't stay off them."

I started edging away, and he said: "I'm sorry, old boy. It's hard for an outsider to understand. You see, I rented this beautiful villa at Cap Ferrat. It overlooks the sea and when I rented it I understood that the sea front belonged to me, that I could enjoy it in privacy and get the vacation I so richly deserved. But in France the law says the public is entitled to use the sea front and they've been squatting in front of my villa every day. They've made me into a shaking, gibbering idiot. But they're my rocks. You understand that, old boy, don't you?"

I said I thought I did.

"Look at it from my point of view," he continued. "I wake up in the morning and I see the sun streaming in. I say to myself, 'What a beautiful—I wonder who are on my rocks,' and I dash out in a rage. Sure enough, there are six people squatting on the concrete slab I had made, with a chain which has a sign with PRIVÉ on it. I say to them: 'I'm sorry, this is private.'

"Then they say: 'You're a foreigner, aren't you?'

"I admit I am.

"Then they say: 'You don't know the laws of France. The sea is for everyone.'

"I then tell them: 'Well, get off my land and get into the sea.'

" 'Ah ha,' they sneer, 'three meters of the land bordering the sea also belongs to the people. So we're entitled to sit here.'

"By this time," Mr. Niven said, "I'm ready to pull my trump card. 'Apparently,' I tell them, 'you are not familiar with the laws of the Quartier of St. Hospice.'

"They look groggy and I press my advantage, making everything up as I go along.

" 'In the Quartier of St. Hospice, owners of villas with their feet in the sea (certain nodding sets in) are allowed to improve a certain percentage of rocks in front of the villas. This is done by pouring cement on the rock, building a dock, and erecting a chain with a sign which says PRIVÉ on it. Once thus improved, the owner of the villa, under the laws of St. Hospice, has the right to rent the improved rocks back from the Quartier of St. Hospice.' Then I pause, having run out of gas. Generally by this time they look shaken, but before they can attack I say: 'If you don't believe me, please feel free to go up to the villa and call the police.'

"That generally does it, and they retreat outside the chain and sit on the spiky uncomfortable rocks, glaring at me as I try to relax eight inches away on my slab of concrete.

"Now the French genius for turning defeat into victory comes into play. They start discussing me among themselves —what a lousy actor I am, how rude all foreigners are, and they comment on my swimming and my figure. I'm forced to hold my stomach in all the time.

"But the worst is lunch time. While I'm lying there they

take out large loaves of bread, cheese, and bottles of wine. I'm starving, but I can't show it. Cries from my own villa announce that luncheon is served, but honor won't permit me to leave.

"They offer me food through the chain like I'm some awful animal in the zoo. But the game forbids me from acknowledging them at all. I have to stay until six, by which time they usually leave and promise to return the next day.

"Now you understand what I've been going through. The rock has become an obsession with me. My whole holiday has been ruined. I don't even know what the villa looks like but I can tell you every periwinkle on the rock and every *oursin* that swims around it.

"I've tried everything," Mr. Niven said, almost close to tears. "I've left air mattresses, flippers, and masks on my rock, but they not only still come on—they use my equipment.

"It's become sort of a club," he said.

"The French won't let foreigners near my rocks, and old-timers, squatters of three weeks or more, resent any new-comers on the rocks. I've more or less gotten to know the old-timers and I probably would be friendly with them by now, but that would be acknowledging defeat, and my regiment would never forgive me.

"But I think the biggest heartbreaker of all is that my sons, brought up in the tradition of Gibraltar, refuse to fight for the rock and would rather go to the public beach and meet some pretty young girls. My wife, a Swede, brought up in an atmosphere of neutrality, also refuses to fight for it. So I'm all alone. All alone— And when I come to an affair such as this I can't even enjoy myself because I know—I just know while I'm drinking champagne and eating lobster, there's someone out there on my rocks having a helluva good time."

Waiting for Nunnally

I HAD lunch with Nunnally Johnson, the American writer, the other day and he claims he's broken the code to avant-garde playwriting.

"I used to specialize in rear-garde and even garde plays," he said, "but I never thought I'd try an avant-garde play until I hit upon the key to the whole thing—an avant-garde play is supposed to show man's inability to communicate in modern society. Well, any writer has difficulty communicating in modern society, but until recently no one took advantage of it.

"But now you can take a bunch of random scenes from different rejected plays, string them together in any order you happen to have them stacked, and before you know it the critics will start comparing you with Beckett, Pinter, Weskett, and Ionesco."

"There must be more to writing an avant-garde play than that," I protested.

"Well, you need a bum," Mr. Johnson said. "Nobody's going to accept an avant-garde play if it doesn't have a bum in it—and the more long-winded he is the better it is for you. But you have to be careful how you introduce your bum— He's got to make a slow entrance so that the character who brings him in has to stop and say: 'Come on, it's all right; they won't hurt you.'

"You bring a bum on early in your first act and you'll have every critic in the house with you, because now they can sit back and relax. They know they're witnessing another dramatization about man's inability to communicate."

"Drama critics like bums?" I said.

"Like them!" Mr. Johnson said. "A bum is to a drama critic what a sad-eyed clown is to a painter. It's money in the bank. All you've got to do is keep your bum talking from 8:45 to

10:45 and there is no way on this earth of your getting a rap.

"You see, the drama critic is absolutely essential to an avant-garde play, just as the art critic is absolutely essential to abstract painting. The drama critic not only explains to readers what the play is all about, he also explains it to the playwright. When I write an avant-garde play and it gets produced I'm sitting pretty, because all I have to do is get the early editions the next morning and find what the hell all that stuff of mine really meant."

I still felt puzzled. "The drama critic is on the side of the author?"

"Of course, he is," Mr. Johnson said. "When you present an intelligible rear-garde or even a garde play, the critic hasn't anything in particular to do but keep awake and then go back to the office and write what he thought about it. But when you write an avant-garde play the critic becomes your collaborator. How can he go back to his typewriter and tell his 500,000 readers he spent an evening in the theater and didn't know what the play was all about?"

"You've got a point," I admitted.

"One of the big hits in London was a play called *The Caretaker*, by Harold Pinter," Mr. Johnson said. "I didn't know what it was all about until a fellow explained it to me: 'Pinter has crystallized it perfectly in that brief scene where the stranger and the owner of the attic admit to each other that they never dream.' Now I ask you, if that isn't the height of noncommunication—what is?"

"But," I said to Mr. Johnson, "what makes you think you can write a better avant-garde play than anybody who is doing it now?"

"I'm going to put more bums in my play than they put in theirs. Because avant-garde plays don't appeal to mass audiences, the producers keep the number of bums down, and they're not really bums—they're actors.

"I'm going to use real bums in my play and pay them off in wine two hours before the curtain goes up. When they get on that stage they're *really* going to be unable to communicate with each other, and the critics are going to go out of their minds."

Olympics for Waiters

A FRIEND of mine, Leonard Louis Levinson, who has written a cookbook called *The Best of Italian Cooking*, wants to organize an Olympics for waiters, in order, as he put it, "to encourage youngsters in what seems to be a dying profession."

"Why did you come to me?"

"Because I'm having trouble talking to French waiters. You see, I learned my French on 33⅓ records and everyone in Paris speaks at 78 r.p.m."

"What are some of the events you would like to include in the waiters' Olympics?" I asked him.

"Well, the most important is the Non-Recognition Event. How long can a waiter ignore a customer before coming over to his table? The event would have to be broken down into several parts.

"There would be a heat in which they would have to ignore the snapping of fingers, one which would include the waving of hands, one where they would refuse to recognize vocal attempts to get their attention, and the finals, in which coins would be dropped on the floor. The waiter who holds his ground longest would win."

Next to the Non-Recognition Event, Mr. Levinson proposes a contest that would be called Whisking the Plate Away. In this one, waiters would compete at whisking a plate away from a customer while he is still eating.

"Proud though I am of our own American waiters, " Mr. Levinson said, "I'll still put my money on an Italian waiter I met in Naples who whisked my minestrone away from me before I had a chance to put any grated cheese on it."

Another event that Mr. Levinson thinks should be included is the Wine Waiter Competition, in which the sommelier is timed to see how soon after a customer's bottom touches a chair he can arrive at the table and ask what wine the people wish to order.

Mr. Levinson added: "Then, of course, there would be the Point-Killing Contest—a gold medal to be given to the waiter who can kill a story better than anybody else."

"But how would you judge such an event?"

"We would have a machine measuring the apoplexy of the person telling the story. The waiter achieving the highest apoplexy of a customer wins."

Mr. Levinson also thinks there should be a Check-Waiting Contest.

"I would break this event up into two parts," he said. "The first part would be clocked on the basis of how long a waiter takes before he brings the check, and the second part would be how fast he can get the customer to pay it before giving him a chance to add it up. I think French waiters have a strong chance in this event."

Mr. Levinson said he has some other competitions in store, including Napkin Flicking, Menu Grabbing, and Soup Spilling.

He also would like to sponsor a race for headwaiters. The headwaiters would race each other walking backward between an obstacle course of tables, with one finger beckoning the customer as they go along.

"What makes a waiters' Olympics really worth while," Mr. Levinson said, "is that every nationality thinks its country's waiters are the best in these events. This will give us a chance to see who really excels at what.

"Everyone's got a waiter they would like to enter, so I don't think there is any problem getting enough contestants."

"Well, then, what is the problem?" I asked.

"I can't get the check from the waiter so I can start getting it organized."

A Sure Weight Loser

THE problem of losing weight is always a serious one and everyone thinks he has a sure-fire system of doing it. The best system I've heard so far was developed by a friend of mine, Bill Morrow, who is Bing Crosby's writer.

Mr. Morrow, now visiting Paris, hit upon it accidentally and over a bad lunch he told me about it.

"A couple of years ago I was in Paris," he said, "tilting the scales around 189 pounds, when I wandered into a bad restaurant and was served one of the worst meals of my life. I left, infuriated, but the next morning I weighed myself and discovered I had lost two pounds. The secret of losing weight, I decided, was to find bad restaurants and eat nowhere else.

"The first thing I did was to find an ex-inspector from the *Guide Michelin*, who had been fired for recommending bad restaurants, and I bought the guide's reject list from him. With this as a starter, I made the rounds, picking up names of other bad restaurants from the owners of the bad restaurants I visited.

"The ideal restaurant for someone trying to lose weight is one where the food is horrible, the waiters are insolent, and the service is awful. If you have all these elements you can lose one to two pounds a meal.

"Sometimes, of course, you might make a mistake, and what has been recommended as a bad restaurant turns out to be a good one. In that case you can save the day by asking for a bad waiter. A bad waiter can always ruin a good meal.

"The thing to always be on guard against is a good restaurant with a good waiter. If this happens, you must leave immediately."

Mr. Morrow is not one to keep something like this to himself. Like most people on diets, he wants to pass on the good word to everyone else. He even decided to form an organization called the Jack Sprat Society.

"It is a kind of John Birch Society for people on diets," he said. "We make up lists of bad restaurants, bad waiters, and even bad recipes, if we can pry them away from the cooks.

"If someone is going to Rome, for example, they might call us up and ask us to recommend ten bad restaurants with credit-card privileges. We'll give them the list, favoring out-of-the-way places which are badly lit, impossible to find, and not worth it once you get there."

Finding bad waiters is a little harder than finding bad restaurants. Mr. Morrow has a list which he refers to when he's giving a party at home. "All my parties are catered by obnoxious waiters who are expert appetite killers."

Mr. Morrow says that if you find a bad waiter in a restaurant you should always tip him well so that he knows that bad service pays.

"Suppose," I said, "you're going to a friend's house for dinner. How do you stay on your diet?"

"Quite simple," he said. "I buy some bad foie gras in a store, and present it to my hostess, who is obligated to serve it in place of the course she planned. Since the foie gras is inedible, I not only lose my appetite for that, but also for the rest of the meal."

Mr. Morrow said he hopes someday to set up a chain of bad restaurants catering to people who are trying to lose weight.

"No matter what you order," Mr. Morrow said, "we'll see that you get the wrong dish, and we'll refuse to change it for you."

"Suppose you come into a town and you don't know a bad restaurant from a good one," I asked. "How can you keep from making a mistake?"

"If you arrive in a strange town," he said, "and you're in doubt, always ask a taxi driver, He's bound to recommend a bad one where he gets a 20 per cent rebate on your check."

Mort Sahl in Paris

MORT SAHL, the American comedian, who did a television show in London for the BBC, stopped off in Paris on his way to he-didn't-know-where.

"It's the first time I've had the time and the money to go somewhere, and I don't know where to go. How about Air France?"

"What about Air France?"

"I don't know. Just how about it?"

"Yeh," I said.

He looked pensive. "That's what I thought."

We were sitting at Fouquet's watching the people go by. I waited for him to speak.

"Listen," he finally said, "the real reason I came to Paris was to visit the museum that has the Aston Martin that once belonged to Françoise Sagan."

I said I'd check into it for him. Then we remained silent for a while watching the pretty girls and their escorts walking up and down the Champs Elysées. He said:

"The trouble is you can't make out in this town without a uniform."

"How was it in London?" I asked him.

"It was a boot. Never saw so many reporters in my life. As I was leaving the airport to come to Paris one of the reporters said to me: 'It's nice to see you without your entourage.' I said: 'I have no entourage. All those people in my suite were your British newspapermen.'

"But the British press is very nice. Like in America they ask you questions about Kennedy and the White House and stuff like that. But in England it's different. When a American comes over they ask him: 'Why did you imprison Ezra Pound?'

"Yuri Gagarin was there when I was there, but I refused

to wave at him. I explained to all my British friends that I was an Alan Shepard man myself.

"It's interesting, the attitudes toward astronauts. In America when Kennedy met Shepard for the first time he shook his hand, but when Khrushchev met Gagarin for the first time he threw his arms around him and kissed him. But the question is, does Khrushchev respect him? Right?"

"Right," I said.

"Everyone is so critical of NATO, but I think it's working very well, at least where the British are concerned. The United States supplies Great Britain with the Polaris submarines and the British supply students to picket them.

"But the British are doing good work. Take Kuwait. You know they have signs up now: 'Enlist in the Army at your friendly Gulf Petrol Station.'"

There were no pretty girls walking for the moment so we both started staring at cars.

"The Germans make the best cars," Sahl said.

I didn't want to get in an argument with him so I asked him why.

"Because they put the motor in the back. In that way when there's an accident the passengers may be impaled, but the engine is protected. Right?"

"Right."

The girls started walking by again. Sahl kept staring at them and then said: "Paris looks like National Hair Week."

Then he said: "I should have stayed in Malibu Beach. I'd be lying on the sand now reading *U.S. News and World Report* and then this volleyball would come my way and I'd throw it back and meet this beautiful heiress who was lonely —aw, the hell with it."

"You don't seem to be having much fun," I said.

"Oh, I wouldn't say that."

"Well, why don't you go shopping?"

"For whom?" he asked.

"Well, if for nobody else, why not your mother?"

"What's the use? It's too late to win her over now."

A New Christmas

IT WAS probably one of the most important meetings of the year. Everyone had been called up to the executive suite on the ninety-seventh floor—well, almost everyone. They hadn't invited the person most concerned.

Carlton was presiding. "Gentlemen, you all know why we're here. I'm now going to turn over the meeting to Mr. MacGuire, of the business management consulting firm of MacGuire, MacGuire and MacGuire, who has been working on the problem for the last eighteen months. Mr. MacGuire."

MacGuire stood up and took several reports out of his briefcase. An assistant passed them around to everyone at the table.

"Gentlemen," he said, "MacGuire, MacGuire and MacGuire were hired to make a study of Christmas. We were given a free hand on this project, and we were asked to make recommendations as to how we could modernize Christmas, cut costs, and at the same time still keep the image that the public has become used to concerning this important children's holiday.

"Now if you will turn to page fifteen you will see a graph showing department store sales, which have been rising every year, and you will notice 1961 broke all records. Yet, despite sales, the margin of profit has been less. After a careful study of all operations concerning Christmas, we believe we have found the bottleneck. It's Santa Claus."

Everyone started talking at once, and Carlton had to rap his gavel for order.

MacGuire continued: "Despite all the modern methods of transportation, you people are still depending on an old man in a sled with reindeer to deliver your parcels. This is not only expensive but wasteful. In many cases we found Mr. Claus had left the wrong gifts in the wrong fireplaces, which resulted in parents bringing them back the next week for costly exchanges.

"We also discovered that because of the lack of space on his sled Santa Claus was not delivering all the toys that parents could buy. Furthermore, our studies showed that a man of his age was a dangerous risk as far as Christmas deliveries went.

"If he had a heart attack or caught pneumonia, it would be too late to substitute another method of distribution, and you would lose millions of dollars."

"He's never been sick before," O'Donnell, the merchandising manager, said.

MacGuire looked at him coldly. "Mr. Claus is an old man, and he doesn't belong in the modern world of business."

Fenton, the advertising manager, said: "That may be true, but he's a helluva image to a lot of kids. You put him out to pasture and we may lose the best merchandising gimmick we've got."

MacGuire said: "I think it's just a question of education. We've sold the kids on Santa Claus, now we can unsell them. We could point out that without Santa Claus they could get a lot more toys; that he is in fact a threat to them, because in the past if they were not good they were told Santa Claus, wouldn't bring them any presents. By eliminating Santa Claus, the middleman, they don't have to worry about their behavior, and they have no one but their parents to blame if they don't get enough toys on Christmas Day. In brief, gentlemen, I suggest we make Santa Claus the heavy."

One of the chief buyers said: "This will be quite a blow to the old fellow. He lives for Christmas Eve."

"There is no reason to let sentiment enter into this," Carlton said. "If Santa Claus is slowing us down, we've got to find some other way of getting out our goods."

"Well," said the personnel manager, "if you're not going to use Santa Claus, how do you propose to deliver the packages on Christmas Eve?"

MacGuire nodded to his assistant who rolled in a long object on a trailer. MacGuire tore off the canvas covering.

"This, gentlemen, is a Christmas missile. As you can see, it has a nose cone which can be filled with packages. Below the cone is a booster, and down here is a radio control. We can send a missile down any chimney in any part of the world. The delivery time is less than two minutes, and we can recover the missiles the day after Christmas and use them again next year. By firing off Christmas missiles at the rate of a thousand every ten seconds, our deliveries will be safe, fast, and dependable, with a payload ten times anything Santa Claus has been able to deliver in the past."

The men all gathered around the missile and looked at it with awe.

"What will we do about Santa Claus?" the merchandising manager asked.

"Give him a pension and make him sign an agreement he won't ever use his influence with children again."

Just then the phone rang. It was a call for the labor relations manager. The manager talked for five minutes and hung up. "That was the Teamsters' Union. They just heard about the Christmas missile and they told us to pack it. They said Santa Claus works or there is no Christmas."

"I knew it," said Carlton, raging mad. "You try to do anything new in this business and the unions will stop you every time."

A.B. of the N.Y.H.T.

A LOT of people think all a newspaperman has to do is sit around and wait for people to come into his office and bribe him. Well, it's true.

Just the other day I received a mysterious call from a woman who said in English she had to see me right away.

When I asked her the nature of her business she said it was too confidential to discuss over the phone.

"Then," I said, "please come over to my confidential office and let's talk."

The lady showed up in an hour. The first thing she wanted to know was if my secretary could hear us. I assured her my secretary couldn't. She then checked the doors and then the window. All was clear.

"I'm not going to beat around the bush," she said. "You're an honest man and therefore I can speak to you frankly. I represent an English tailor in Paris and we would like you to write an article about us, and in exchange we will clothe you for nothing."

"Oh, I couldn't do that," I said. (I always say that at the beginning when someone is trying to bribe me, because it sounds good.)

The lady seemed annoyed. "Mr. Buchwald, this is not a bribe, and you shouldn't consider it a bribe. This is a straightforward business proposition. We clothe some of the best people in Paris. You would be amazed if I told you their names. I can't, but I can give you their initials. We clothe C.d.G."

"Not big C.d.G.?"

She nodded. "Sometimes known as General C.d.G."

"Is he also known sometimes as President C.d.G.?"

"Yes," she said. "He is."

"I have no idea who you mean."

"Never mind," she said. "The point is, we're after the American trade, and you can help us."

"But I'm not allowed to mention the name of any commercial firm in my articles," I told her, "unless it's an air line, an advertiser, or both."

She said: "Look. Blank Blank is the finest tailor in Paris. J.F.K. once had a suit made by him."

"J.F.K. of Hyannis Port and Washington, D.C.?"

"And Palm Beach, Florida," she said.

"The one who was in Vienna meeting with N.S.K. of Moscow?"

"The very one."

"I never heard of him."

She tried again. "Now you listen to me. Even if you don't write an article about us, we still want to clothe you. All you have to do in exchange is when someone comes to Paris and wants to buy a suit, send them to us. You have very influential friends, don't you?"

"Well, I know D.F.Z. of Twentieth Century-F., and H.R.L. of *T.L.*, *Fortune*, and *Sports Illustrated*. But I don't think they'd listen to me if I told them where to buy a suit."

"All right. Now I'm going to be very frank with you," she said. "I notice what you're wearing, and I must say it's disgraceful for a man in your position to be walking around like that. We will clothe you absolutely free. You won't have to write about us, you won't have to send us any friends, you don't even have to wear our label. All we ask is that you allow us to say you have your suits made by us."

"The answer is no," I said. "And it's not because I'm afraid. But if you go around saying A.B. of the N.Y.H.T. has his suits made by you, other tailors will start coming in and I'll be so busy having fittings I won't be able to see people who want to shoe me, hat me, or shirt me for the winter. I have enough suits. It's the accessories that are keeping me down."

A Confusing Week

I'M IN the middle of a very busy week, so much so that I haven't had a chance to do much work. What happened was that the American magazine *Look* said they would like to do a picture story on me, on how I live and work in Paris, and naturally I was delighted. *Look* has at least eight million readers, not counting people who pick it up in barbershops and beauty parlors and my mother-in-law, who is a subscriber, so it was hard to say no. *Look* sent over from the United States two of their top men, Jack Star, a reporter, and Douglas Kirkland, a photographer, and I agreed they could follow me around night and day taking pictures and interviewing me while I interviewed other people. At the time I didn't realize how confusing it could be.

The truth is I live a very quiet life in Paris. In the morning I come in and read the mail, dictate a few letters to Ursula under pseudonyms, requesting that the editor rerun my Thanksgiving Day column, then I play gin rummy with a fellow down the hall, then I go to lunch with the fellow I played gin rummy with, then I take a nap, then I write an article, then I go home and read *France-soir* to find out what happened in Paris that day.

There is rarely any variance in this routine, but obviously this wasn't what *Look* had in mind, so I had to change my entire schedule.

For a starter I had to impress the *Look* men with the fact that I really lead a glamorous life. The first thing I did was go out to a movie studio in Paris and say hello to Henry Fonda, Edmund O'Brien, and Darryl Zanuck, who were making *The Longest Day*.

It was too difficult to explain what I was doing with a writer and a photographer, so I didn't say anything other than to introduce them as members of the *Look* staff.

But as I talked to Mr. Fonda and Mr. O'Brien, the photographer started taking pictures of me with the stars' backs to the camera, and Mr. Star was taking notes of the questions I was asking the actors instead of their answers.

Finally I told the actors what was going on. The press agent immediately called *his* photographer in to take pictures of Mr. Kirkland taking pictures of me being interviewed while I interviewed Mr. Fonda, Mr. O'Brien, and Mr. Zanuck. It caused a bit of confusion on the set as no one knew who was taking what of whom.

On the way out of the studio I had the good fortune to

bump into Gene Kelly, whom I stopped and chatted with while Mr. Kirkland shot pictures and Mr. Star took notes.

Mr. Kelly became nervous, so I had to let go of his hand which I was shaking vigorously so Mr. Kirkland could see I really knew important people in Paris.

Next day I had a more serious problem. Mr. Fonda, Mr. O'Brien, Mr. Zanuck, and Mr. Kelly were the only celebrities I knew who were in Paris, and I still had nine days to go.

I called up Irwin Shaw, the writer, and told him *Look* was doing a story on me and asked him if he would come to lunch so we could be photographed together.

"I'd like to," he replied, "but I'm playing tennis."

"Well, could they take a picture of us playing tennis together?" I asked.

Mr. Shaw said: "You don't play tennis."

"I don't do anything they're taking pictures of me doing," I cried.

But Mr. Shaw said he had an important game and, besides, he photographed very badly from the back.

So I had my picture taken with an industrial designer from Lausanne and Bing Crosby's agent, whom I met by luck in the lobby of the Hotel George V where I was waiting to be photographed with *anyone* who came in. Tuesday night I had my picture taken with a stripteaser at the Crazy Horse Saloon, several students dancing the Twist, and Raymond Oliver cooking at the Grand Véfour.

Now all I have to worry about is Wednesday.

Good News, Big Guys

THE world judo championships, which were held in Paris, dashed one of the most popular conceptions of this increasingly popular sport: that is, that a little guy could beat a big guy. It turns out that it just isn't true any more. Even in judo a good big guy can beat a good little guy, and that should be good news for good big guys everywhere.

For years, thanks to judo, good big guys have been afraid of good little guys, because the big guys were told the little guys could use the big guy's own weight to defeat them. When a little guy walked into a bar, the big guys edged away from him in fear that the little guy would start an argument. Little guys used to steal girls away from big guys because the big guys were afraid if they protested they'd get their arms broken. The more popular judo became, the more belligerent the little guys became.

In Paris, for example, where the sport has been very popular, the most frightening thing to see was an argument over a traffic accident in which a little guy and a big guy were involved. The little guy would jump out of his automobile, and when the big guy saw how little the little guy was, he would cringe in his seat and shake with terror.

That's the way it's been for years. But the last judo championships changed all this. A big guy, a six-foot-seven, 240-pound Dutchman named Anton Geesink, won the world judo championship, defeating the best Japanese and Korean stars and dramatically, in one flip, changing the entire principle of judo. He proved conclusively that a big guy can still beat a little guy at his own game, and it's a warning to all little guys to leave us big guys alone.

Judo as a sport is quite different from judo as a form of defense usually taught to girls who have to walk home late at night by themselves.

In the sport the contestants, wearing loose jackets and loose pants, face each other on a mat. Then they grab each other's jackets, pulling and pushing until one or the other is off balance. At this moment, using the weight of the other, and a technique which takes years to learn, one contestant tries to throw the other contestant down on the mat.

The philosophy of the sport is not to attack your opponent, but to let him make the move that you take advantage of. For years a man's weight worked against him because no one thought a big guy had the reflexes of a little guy, and reflexes are what count. In fact, big guys avoided the sport because they were afraid of being made fools of by little guys (or women who walked home late at night).

But a few years ago, by accident, a big guy in Japan was goaded into a match with a little guy, and by sheer power tossed him across the room. When other big guys heard about this they all rushed to learn the sport. The little guys kept developing techniques to thwart the big guys, but the big guys started learning techniques of their own and suddenly technique plus power was defeating technique alone.

A tearful little guy, a judo expert, whom I interviewed after the championship match, said: "We knew it would happen sooner or later. We knew big guys with power and technique could beat little guys, but *they* didn't know it. Now that they've proven it with Geesink, every country is going to start developing judo teams made up of big guys. It was our sport, the only sport the little guy excelled in over the big guy and now that's gone."

I started pushing him around just to see what he would do, but instead of defending himself all he said was, "Why don't you pick on somebody your own size?"

3.
Is It Safe To Be
an American?

We Like the Image

THE HONORABLE ED MURROW
UNITED STATES INFORMATION AGENCY
WASHINGTON, D.C.

Dear Ed,

I see you made a speech out in Hollywood to a group of film-industry leaders in which you took them to task for the type of movie they were exporting abroad. You were quoted as saying that American movies give a false picture of American life—that foreign moviegoers have come to believe "that Chicago is still wracked by gang warfare, that the West is still wild and we're still killing Indians, and that any woman without a 40-inch bust . . . must *not* be an American."

Now frankly, Ed, what's wrong with this image of the United States? The foreign moviegoer gets great pleasure in thinking that Chicago is full of gangsters, because if we've got them all in one city the rest of the country must be clean.

Besides, it's better to fool them into thinking Chicago is full of gangsters than to let them know the truth—that the Denver police department is full of crooks.

As for our Westerns, there is probably nothing in the world that makes a foreigner feel warmer toward the United States than a good shoot-em-up. It isn't a question of showing cowboys killing Indians, because everyone knows the trend in Westerns these days is to kill more white men than redskins so you won't get in racial trouble at the box office, but there is nothing a foreigner admires more than a man who is fast on the draw and tall in the saddle and who gets the girl at the end.

That's the perfect image of an American, and let's not louse

105

it up, particularly since we're trying to attract all those female tourists to the United States.

As for your remarks about foreigners thinking all American women have 40-inch busts, for heaven's sake, Ed, that is the greatest image in the world for America. There isn't a country on the face of the globe whose citizens don't envy a big-busted woman. I've heard foreigners say a lot of things about Americans, but I never heard them complain about the size of the American female chest. Forty-inch busts are what European men's dreams are made of, and it would be a pity if we did anything to disturb their illusions.

If you really want to do something, I think you should ban sending American fashion magazines such as *Vogue, Harper's Bazaar,* and *Mademoiselle* abroad, because when foreigners see the busts on the models in those publications they start to wonder if we really do have the secret of the 40-inch bust, as our motion pictures claim we do.

The big problem as I see it, Ed, is not that the world has the wrong image of Americans but that pretty soon they won't have any image at all. In Europe, now that the European Common Market is under way, the policy is not any longer to dislike Americans, but to *ignore* them completely. This is far more ignominious than being hated. Anyone can rationalize being scorned, but how can anyone explain being ignored? Therefore we've got a lot of work to do, not so much in being liked, as in getting mentioned in any context at all.

As a starter I suggest Americans go around Europe painting U.S. GO HOME signs on the walls, so at least the Europeans will know we're still there.

Justifying Expenses

REPORTS out of Washington indicate that American foreign service officers will have to justify their entertainment of foreign officials before they can get the money to pay for it.

In the past a foreign service officer received a certain amount of money for entertainment purposes at the beginning of the year. But under a new system announced by William Crockett, Assistant Secretary of State, the officer will have to explain how he spent the money, presumably to a committee which will evaluate each voucher to see that the money is used properly.

The reason for the new order is, presumably, pressure from Congressman Rooney of the Appropriations Committee, whose pet peeve has always been representation allowances for American Embassies abroad, which some Congressmen have dubbed "booze funds" for the want of a better name.

Some people may say this is pretty hard on American diplomats who are trying to do their jobs, but I'm in sympathy with Congressman Rooney. After all, if you're going to give $300,000,000 to Laos, a billion dollars to Chiang Kai-shek, and so forth, you have to make economies somewhere, and what better place to start than canceling a $200 cocktail party before it gets started.

I can just imagine an expense-evaluation meeting once the new policy goes into effect:

The committee is seated in the conference room of an American embassy, and the chairman tells the secretary to send a foreign service officer in. The officer enters nervously as the committee stares at him.

The chairman studies the officer's expense account.

"Ruggerbottom," he addresses the officer, "we'd like to ask you a few questions."

"Yes, gentlemen."

"You have down here on your expense account 'Lunch for two $10.50.' Would you kindly tell us whom you took to lunch?"

"It was a Romanian double agent," Ruggerbottom answers. "He gave me the minutes of a meeting between all the heads of the satellite countries held in Moscow last week. No one knew what had taken place at the meeting and I cabled the report to Washington immediately."

"And you had to take him to lunch for that?" one of the committee members asks incredulously. "You couldn't have gotten the same information by asking him to come to the embassy?"

"No, he didn't want to be seen at the embassy. It would have compromised his position."

Another committee member asks: "Why couldn't you have met in the park?"

"He was hungry," Ruggerbottom replies.

The committee chairman snaps: "That's no excuse. If we fed every hungry double agent, the State Department would go broke. You'll have to pay for the lunch yourself. Now the next item, 'Train fare $6.80.' Can you justify that?"

"Yes, sir. I had to take a train to meet an Estonian refugee who smuggled out the blueprints of a new Russian nuclear submarine."

"Why couldn't he have mailed it to you?"

"I was afraid it would get lost," Ruggerbottom protests.

"But you weren't afraid of the $6.80 being lost, were you?" the chairman says as he writes "Expense unjustified."

One of the committee members says: "Ask him about the bar bill for $9.50."

The chairman: "I'm coming to that."

Ruggerbottom speaks up. "I had a drink with the Foreign Minister to discuss the new reciprocal trade agreement. We had a bottle of champagne and—"

"I thought as much!" a committee member shouts. "You don't care how you spend the money, do you? Do you realize the Foreign Minister might be out in six months? Then what good is the champagne?"

The chairman says: "Ruggerbottom, you could have achieved the same ends over a glass of beer. You'll have to pay the $9.50 yourself."

"Is that all, sir?" Ruggerbottom asks.

"Not by a long shot," the chairman says sternly. "You have down here 'cocktails, dinner, and night club $230.' Will you be so kind as to tell this committee just exactly whom you entertained for $230?"

Ruggerbottom answers: "It was a congressman and his wife from the House Appropriations Committee. They said they wanted to see the town and I took them . . ."

The chairman interrupts: "You don't have to go any further. Your explanation is perfectly satisfactory. Congratulations, we accept the $230 expense unanimously." The committeemen all shout their approval.

"That will be all for now, Ruggerbottom. But watch your step with those other expenses. After all, there's just so much money in the till and we have to use it wisely."

Nondeductible Wives

CONGRESS is wrestling with a new tax law which is supposed to tighten up on existing entertainment tax write-offs for business purposes. In the future you may have trouble writing off as a business tax deduction a yacht, a hunting lodge, or even a trip to a foreign land, if it's proved you got any fun out of it yourself.

While most people are sympathetic with abolishing the larger tax excesses, there is one rider to the new law that might very well wreck the American home. And that is that a wife can no longer be considered tax-deductible.

If, for example, you take a client and *his* wife to dinner and the theater, you can deduct them as legitimate business write-offs. You can also deduct yourself. But if the new law is passed, you can't deduct your wife.

So obviously no man in his right fiscal mind is going to want to take his wife out to dinner any more.

What makes the new law even more aggravating from a wife's point of view is that her husband can take out another woman on his expense account, provided the other woman has something to do with his business. This makes it much more attractive for a man to take out a beautiful blonde stranger, who works in a similar business and is considered deductible, than his own wife, who is really nothing more than a financial drain on his income-tax return.

One shudders to think what will happen to the American home if the law is passed.

The husband is shaving and whistling in the bathroom, getting ready to go out for the evening. His wife, still in her apron, is sitting wistfully on the bed watching him.

"Where are you going tonight?" she asks him.

"We'll probably go to *Camelot* and then to the Persian Room afterward."

"Who are you going with?"

"The woman buyer of lingerie from Sears Roebuck."

The wife starts sniffling.

"Now don't start that again," the husband says. "You know very well why you can't go. Do you want my accountant to explain it to you again?"

"I haven't been out in three months."

"You're exaggerating. You went out seven weeks ago with me when that man from the Aetna Curtain Company took us to a hockey game at Madison Square Garden."

"Something's happened to us," the wife says. "We used to have so much fun doing things together."

"Blame it on Uncle Sam," the husband says. "When I married you you were the most beautiful legitimate write-off a man could want. I'll never forget that first night when I took you to the Copacabana. The bill came to forty-five dollars and we both laughed as I signed the check. Do you know how much I'd have to earn now to pay that check? One hundred and fifty dollars."

"Then you married me just because I was tax-deductible?" the wife says.

"Now you're being unreasonable," the husband says angrily. "I married you because I loved you. I took you *out* because you were deductible. Don't you see the difference? Look, if it was up to me I'd take you out every night in the week. But

if I did we wouldn't be able to live on the salary I'm making."

"Well, why are you always going out if I can't go out with you?" the wife sobs.

"Because I can deduct myself. It doesn't cost me anything if I go out. Darling, you've got to grow up and face facts as they are. I'll tell you what you do. Write another letter to your congressman. Maybe by the time I get back from Florida they'll change the law."

"Florida?"

"Oh, I forgot to tell you. . . ."

Why I Resigned

Now that Major General Edwin A. Walker has resigned from the Army, the truth can be told as to why I left the United States Marine Corps in 1945, only sixteen years before retirement. I resigned because I was admonished and removed from command of a barbershop cleaning detail at Cherry Point, North Carolina, when I tried to indoctrinate my men in the politics in which I believe and which I believed my men should believe.

The Navy Department saw fit to criticize me for these actions and wanted to transfer me to command of a salt-water shower detail in Hawaii. But rather than work under little men, who in the name of the country punish loyal service to it, I decided to leave the Marines and forfeit all the benefits I had built up in my four years as a Pfc, to do what I found it impossible to do in uniform.

Early in my career I discovered my first sergeant was a Communist, my commanding officer was a Communist, the commander of the base was a Communist, the Secretary of the Navy was a Communist, and the President of the United States as well as all members of Congress were Reds. I felt I had to impart this information to my men, as they thought the enemy was the Japanese, when in fact the real enemy was not the people we were fighting, but the people at home who had infiltrated all the high places of government.

I tried to speak out against these people. I tried to tell my men to vote against them in the elections. I tried to show them that a democracy could survive only with a strong military government in command of the situation—and for this I was censured and my rights encroached on by the executive branch of the government, which criticized me for speaking the truth in accordance with my conviction and conscience.

In defeat it turned out I was in good company.

Ten million men in the armed services quit at the same time I did, mostly because they couldn't stomach being censured and ordered around by little men.

There is no use going into the details of my court-martial. All I said while sweeping up hair in the barbershop was that my first sergeant had a beer bottle for a head and a gas bag for a stomach. I didn't realize he was getting a shave at the time.

In typical Communist fashion, he took exception to this description, and I decided the best thing to do was leave the service and go into civilian life where I could express these opinions without fear of getting thirty days' mess duty.

So my sympathies are with Major General Walker. I know how hard it is to say what you want to say in the military, because even in a military barbershop there can be subversive elements ready to discourage anyone who wants to communicate his ideas to men under his command.

Now that General Walker doesn't have any military duties he can hunt Communists to his heart's content. The first place I always look is under my bed.

Semper Fidelis, Sir

As a FORMER member of the United States Marine Corps who served in the troubles of World War II, I would like to raise my voice in protest from the Halls of Montezuma to the Shores of Tripoli over Senator Strom Thurmond's dastardly attempt to give a "cross-section" of Marines an "intelligence" test on aspects of the cold war.

Anyone who has ever had anything to do with the Marines knows that they are not interested in the President of the Soviet Presidium, the difference between civil rights and the Communist Party, the identification of Moise Tshombe, and the question of dialectical materialism.

As a matter of fact, when I was in boot camp at Parris Island, I was given an intelligence test by my drill instructor. The indoctrination was thorough, and if I know the Marines, I'm sure it hasn't changed much.

These were some of the questions, and the answers that were drilled into us night after night to make us fighting men.

"What is your rifle number?" the drill sergeant asked

"280311," I replied, standing at attention.

"Who are you?"

"I am dirt but someday I hope to be a Marine, though I am a fool to think I shall ever achieve such an honor."

"Who am I?"

"You are God. You are my father, my mother, you are the only one I fear, and I kiss the parade ground you walk on."

"Who is the enemy we are fighting?"

"The U.S. Army, which gets all the easy jobs while the U.S. Marines have to do the dirty work. We go in first and then they come later and get all the glory."

"What do you call the enemy?"

"Dogfaces."

"Next to the Dogfaces who is the other enemy we are fighting to preserve a free world?"

"The U.S. Navy, otherwise known as Swab Jockeys, who are always trying to get the Marines on the beach first, so the Navy will get the glory."

"What is a Marine valued at?"

"The current rate of exchange is one Marine is worth one

hundred Dogfaces and one hundred Swab Jockeys. It never changes from action to action."

"Identify the following: General Douglas MacArthur."

"He is a no-good Dogface general who is always trying to steal the glory away from the Marine Corps."

"Who is General Eisenhower?"

"He's some guy fighting some minor skirmish in Europe that has nothing to do with the real war in the Pacific."

"Who is President Roosevelt?"

"He is the man who uses the Marine Corps band at all official functions."

"What is the role of a Marine?"

"To obey without question everything his sergeant tells him, to guard his post until properly relieved, and to fight for the corps on land, on sea, and in any bar he happens to be in."

"Why did you join the Marine Corps?"

"To steal girls away from Dogfaces and Swab Jockeys."

"Who is the greatest fighting man you know?"

"You are, and I only hope that someday I can lick your boots."

"Why are you fighting for your country?"

"Because you told me to fight for it."

"Very good. Now let me ask you one crucial question. Who are the Japs?"

"Huh?"

"Huh, what?"

"Huh, sir."

An Ex-Pfc Comes Home

THEY laughed at me eighteen years ago when as a poor Marine Pfc I vowed someday I'd sleep in the captain's cabin aboard a Navy aircraft carrier. But they aren't laughing any more. Last week I went out on a cruise, the USS *Independence,* and damned if that wasn't where I slept. (The captain was up on the bridge for the entire trip, in case any of you are wondering where *he* slept.)

The USS *Independence* is part of the Sixth Fleet, which operates in the Mediterranean. As it was explained to me by some young Naval fighter pilots, the *Independence* has two missions. One is to sail about as an instrument of good will, calling at different ports and making friends with our allies. The second mission of the carrier, according to the pilots, is to prove that there really is no need for the United States Air Force. Given more carriers, the Navy could do the job of defending Europe at half the price with twice the payload.

The pilots pointed out that if it wasn't for carriers like the USS *Independence,* the Air Force would have wiped out the Navy long ago. But with the carrier deterrent, the SAC bombers will never attack, because the Air Force knows that if the balloon goes up the Navy will be able to wipe out the Pentagon before the Air Force can knock out Naval headquarters in Washington.

The USS *Independence* is one of the largest ships in the world. She weighs 60,000 tons, is a quarter mile long, and sleeps 4,000 men, and the flight deck is as large as the Principality of Monaco, though not as hilly.

She has every kind of plane on her from helicopters to heavy attack bombers, which carry nuclear warheads which nobody talks about.

The value of the carrier with her planes is somewhere in the neighboorhood of $500,000,000.

The captain responsible for this investment earns $13,000 a year, which makes him one of the most underpaid executives in the American free enterprise system.

It's quite an experience to be a guest aboard the USS *Independence.* A civilian is treated like a visiting congressman.

At the dock at Cannes I was met by a lieutenant commander, who escorted me in a special boat out to the carrier, where I was greeted on deck by several commanders, lieutenant commanders, and ensigns, all of whom saluted me as I came up the ladder.

The executive officer, Commander I. M. Rowell, Jr., told me I would be dining that night with Captain Evan P. Aurand and the next evening with Rear Admiral William E. Ellis and his staff. Lieutenant Commander Thomas Wentworth, Jr., was put at my disposal to act as my guide and see that I had a pleasant cruise.

Thinking back eighteen years ago to how it was as a Pfc in the Marines, I started to sob uncontrollably.

It was obvious that through all the years the Navy had felt guilty over the way it treated me, and now it was trying to make up to me. A sailor mopped up the tears as I was escorted to my cabin, where I was given a cup of hot coffee and the key to the bridge in case I got bored and wanted to steer the ship.

If my old Marine First Sergeant Hubba Hubba Fat with Blubba could only see me now!

The hardest thing for me to get used to aboard the USS *Independence* was everyone calling me "sir." It's probably easier than remembering your name, but it's kind of embarrassing, particularly if you keep calling the officers "sir."

For example, when Lieutenant Commander Wentworth was showing me around the ship, he would say:

"Would you like to go up on the hangar deck, sir?"

"Yes, sir," I replied.

"Is there anything in the ship's store you would like to buy, sir?"

"Thank you, sir," I would reply. "There is."

This went on for several hours, and it finally got confusing, so I said to the commander:

"Look, just call me Art."

"Thank you," he replied. "Just call me Tom, sir."

They Take Off Their Hats to Me

THE average person, frustrated by events in the world today, is constantly asking what he can do to feel he has some control over the situation. The answer is quite simple. He can get himself catapulted off a U.S. aircraft carrier in an A3D Skywarrior Heavy Attack Bomber, make a simulated nuclear attack on the enemy, and return to the carrier three hours later, landing at 250 miles an hour. It's amazing how the problems of the world become infinitesimal compared to your own problems of coming back again in one piece.

As a guest of the Sixth Fleet I was invited to participate in a strike exercise and I was offered the fourth seat in a three-seater bomber.

"Everyone on a carrier takes his hat off to someone who flies in an A3D," I was told by the operations officer of the *Independence* as he made me sign four forms releasing the Navy from any responsibility for taking me on the flight.

Before I could ask *why* they took off their hats, I was zipped into a yellow flight suit and then helped into a Mae West lifejacket which contained, among other things, night flares, day flares, a dye marker, a life raft, and a shark chaser, which one of the Tiger pilots explained scares away sharks but attracts barracuda. I was also given a crash helmet, an oxygen mask, and a cup of coffee.

Thus I was ready to be catapulted off the USS *Independence*.

Up on the flight deck I was pushed into the cabin and placed in a parachute which was resting on a tin can, which made up the fourth seat in an A3D. My pilot, Lieutenant Commander Bart Bartholomew, and his crew of two had seats that resembled electric chairs.

Before taking off I was briefed on what to do in case I had "to leave the aircraft without landing."

"It's quite simple," the crewman told me. "Unlatch your chest plate before you pull your toggles on the Mae West. Try to undo your leg straps and get out from under your harness and pull the lever on the safety belt upward at the same time you pull the lever under your seat downward, and don't unhook your oxygen mask or you may not be able to get at your parachute. Have you got it?"

"Yes, sir," I replied. "If anything happens to the plane I'm going to die."

He slapped me on the shoulder and before I knew it we were on the catapult platform waiting to be shot off.

"Going off the Cat," as we bomber pilots like to put it, is quite an experience. It's like being shot out of a cannon while someone is pounding you in the stomach and trying to break your neck at the same time. If the plane has enough power, you go up; if it doesn't, you start sprinkling around your shark repellent.

The plane had enough power, and before I knew it we were up to 10,000 feet. Then before I knew it we were down to 150 feet. Then before I knew it we were up to 10,000 feet, then before I knew it we were down to 150 feet and then before I knew it we were flying over Corsica, then before I knew it we were flying over the *Independence*, then before I knew it we were flying over the cup of coffee they gave me before we had taken off.

The exercise, as it was explained to me, was to sink two destroyers, the island of Sardinia, and all of Italy. The Navy didn't *really* want to sink all these places, but in peacetime you have to take the targets that are available to you.

After three hours they told us we could come back.

The *Independence* from the air looked the size of one of the papers I had signed releasing the Navy from any responsibility in case I didn't make it, and I was waiting for the signal from Lieutenant Commander Bartholomew to jump out and swim to the carrier. But he was being difficult about it and insisted on landing with his plane.

As long as I had gone this far I decided to stay with him,

and so I grabbed the radar man as we came in for the landing.

The heavy bomber, screaming in protest, came down on the deck, and the hook in the back of the plane grabbed the cable. The monster stopped with a groan.

As we taxied away, everyone on the *Independence* took off their hats. It was the most moving sight I had ever seen.

This Is a Happy Ship

THE problem of a giant aircraft carrier is how to keep 4,000 men busy and happy although they are constantly in each other's hair twenty-four hours a day. One of the ways of doing this is to divide the ship up into port and starboard watches. This is how it works. Let's say port personnel have the first watch. What they do is take chains or heavy cables and drag them along the decks over the heads of the starboard-watch people who are trying to sleep. The port watch does this for four hours until it is relieved by the starboard-watch people who start hammering on the decks over the cabins where the port watch is trying to sleep.

In four hours the starboard watch is relieved and this gives the port watch a chance to start up the jet engines over the heads of the starboard watch. When the starboard watch comes on again it checks out the catapulting equipment, which, below decks, sounds like depth charges going off and keeps the port watch hugging the bulkheads.

If for some reason one watch fails to keep the other watch awake, general quarters is sounded over the loud-speaker system, and that means *everyone* has to go to his station.

Since all anyone wants out of life on the USS *Independence* is some sleep, nobody has a chance to think about anything else, and this is why the aircraft carrier is considered a happy ship.

The biggest mistake a visitor can make on the USS *Inde-*

pendence is to ask somebody what certain instruments are for—because they'll tell you.

I made the mistake of wandering into the Combat Information Center, which is a darkened room where men are staring into all sorts of beeping scopes, pushing red buttons, and talking quietly into telephones to other mysterious parts of the ship.

"I suppose all this stuff is top secret?" I asked hopefully of the officer in charge.

"On the contrary," he said; "I would be happy to explain it to you. Here you have the air scope, which gives the air picture on the airstatus board, and there you have the surface scope, which gives the picture on the surface-status board. Now over here you have the three-sector bogey picture handled by three air scopesmen. The sector is watched over by a CIC control officer who will assign an appropriate designation at which time the air-control scope controller then takes over a CAP to attack it and then scratch it. If the CAP splashes the bogey, the CIC officer scratches the bogey on the air picture. But if he doesn't splash the bogey, we set Condition Red, which alerts gunnery and gives them the bearing and angles at ten o'clock."

"That's mighty interesting," I said. "But it sort of takes the fun out of war, doesn't it?"

The officer in charge moved on to the Planned Position Indicator, and I escaped through a Fire Control Umbrella into the chief petty officers' mess, where I was invited for lunch. I told the chiefs I had just seen some very intricate machinery in the CIC Room but I didn't know if I could write about it or not.

"There is only one top-secret machine aboard this here carrier," one of the chiefs drawled, "and that's not topside but below in the laundry. The Navy has perfected a new laundry mangling machine which has a powered lawn mower inside of it so it can cut up your clothes in thirty seconds. Under the old system the Navy laundrymen had to tear your clothes by hand and that took time. Also every once in a while they left a button on your shirt by mistake. But with the new Anti-Laundry Detergent Missile you don't get back any buttons at all."

"What happens to the buttons?" I asked.

"They're used by the machine to shoot holes in your socks."

4.
Is It Safe To Be
in Politics?

The Secret Orlov Plan

THE way for a newspaperman to get reams of mail these days is to write a piece attacking the John Birch Society, General Walker, and any of the extreme right-wing groups which seem to be having a renaissance in the United States.

A recent article suggesting General Walker look under his bed every night if he wanted to find Communists brought in the best batch of mail I've had since I wrote that James Whistler was an orphan and painted somebody else's mother.

The letters in their denunciation seemed to follow a pattern, and I was quite puzzled by it until by accident I found myself in Maxim's sitting next to a Russian named Serge Orlov, who was eating large portions of caviar and drinking vodka.

I got to be friendly and pretty soon, after several vodkas, I asked him what he did.

"I used to be in charge of all Communist subversive activity in the United States," he said.

"You were?" I asked in amazement.

"Yes. Perhaps you have heard of the Orlov Plan?"

I admitted I hadn't, though I explained it was because I hadn't kept up much on subversive activities in the United States recently.

"The Orlov Plan," he said, swigging down another vodka, "was the most masterful subversive plan ever devised in the cold war. I received the Fourth Order of the Lenin Cross for it."

"What was it?" I asked.

"I was in charge of all internal subversion in the United States from 1950 to just a few months ago. For years we had been trying to infiltrate the unions and the liberal groups, but we made little headway. We were wasting our time and money. The U.S. was stronger than ever, its policy toward the Soviets had toughened, and little damage was being done to American morale.

"I realized something had to be done. Then I hit upon it— the Orlov Plan.

"The only people willing to wreck the United States government, I discovered, were the extreme right-wing groups. They were being ignored, and yet they were the key to all internal subversion. I laid out a plan. I would have my agents organize a program working through the extreme right wing which would stand the United States on its head.

"First I would get the right wing to accuse President Eisenhower of being a Communist. Then I would get them to call their own high government officials traitors. Then I would see that the right wing attacked American United Nations representatives. I also would convince the right wing that Russia didn't have atomic weapons.

"Then I would encourage rumors that everyone in the State Department was either a Communist or a homosexual. I gave orders to wreak havoc in the armed services by turning military officers against civilians. I even proposed they impeach Chief Justice Warren of the Supreme Court. I laid out different attacks against anyone who advocated better education or health facilities in the United States. And the topper was that anyone who disagreed with this would be accused of being a card-holding Communist.

"When I proposed the plan in Moscow, the Kremlin thought I was crazy. But they figured they had nothing to lose. Well, you can see the results for yourself. The seeds of doubt about America are being planted by their own people, and we've been making more progress in wrecking the U.S. Constitution in the last few years than my predecessors have been able to do since the revolution."

"Then you mean all these extreme right-wing groups are really Communist dupes?" I asked in surprise.

"Exactly, they're doing the Lord's work for the Soviet Union, and most of them don't even know it."

"But why are you in Paris and why are you telling me all this?" I asked him.

He finished off the bottle of vodka. "Because," he said, "I defected."

"Defected?"

"Yes," he said, smiling. "You see, when I proposed the plan to the Kremlin they asked me how much it would cost. I said for a start about a million dollars, which they turned over to me to dispense. Well, what happened was, when I got the extreme right-wing groups to help me, I discovered they insisted on putting up their own money. It didn't cost me a dime. And those people are loaded. So I just took the million dollars and deposited it in Switzerland. The Soviets heard about it, and I decided I better defect. Anyhow, they still call it the Orlov Plan. If I hadn't swiped the money, I might have been sleeping next to Lenin one of these days."

Happy Birthday to You

You can't pick up a paper these days without reading about some country sending a stiff note to another country concerning some diplomatic matter such as Berlin, Bizerte, Kuwait, or Outer Mongolia. While a great deal of publicity is given to the notes themselves, no one knows who actually writes them or how they are conceived. But it's not hard to guess what happens. Let us suppose we are in Moscow at the Ministry of Foreign Affairs. Mr. Gromyko, the Russian Foreign Minister, picks up the phone and says: "Get me the Stiff Note Department."

It takes a few minutes to get through and Mr. Gromyko is furious.

"Why didn't you answer the phone, Comrade Vladimir?" Mr. Gromyko says angrily.

"I'm sorry, Comrade Minister," Vladimir replies, "I was just rejecting a stiff note from Turkey in no uncertain terms."

"Well, forget about Turkey for a moment," Mr. Gromyko says.

"The Premier wants you to send a stiff note to the United States, France, Great Britain, and West Germany, and he says you might as well scare the hell out of little Denmark while you're at it."

"Is it a new note or a stiff note rejecting one of their stiff notes?" Vladimir wants to know.

"A little of both," Mr. Gromyko replies. "We want you to threaten them with the super bomb, germ warfare, rockets, nuclear warheads, and total annihilation. But, Vladimir, leave room open for negotiation."

"I got it, Comrade Minister. The usual stuff about Western warmongers and their hostile acts, for which they must bear the consequences."

"That's the idea, Vladimir, but don't forget to mention that their previous note concerning Berlin was completely unjustified and their reply to our note, which was a reply to their original stiff note, was an affront to all peace-loving socialist countries."

Vladimir says: "Should I add it as a P.S. or in the main body of our note?"

"Put it in the first paragraph," Mr. Gromyko says. "If they reject the note, which they in all certainty will, they may never get as far as the P.S."

"Is there anything else, Comrade Minister?"

"You might put in a plug for Titov and Gagarin while you're at it. The boys have been off the front pages for a few months and they're getting pretty mad about it."

"While I've got you on the phone, Comrade Minister, we're having a lot of trouble with the stiff note we're sending the West concerning the closing off of East Berlin. No matter how we write it we still can't explain why we had to cut off the city so the East German refugees wouldn't flee."

"But, Comrade Vladimir, I told you to put in the note the

reason we shut off East Berlin was not to keep the East Germans from fleeing to the West, but to keep the West Germans from fleeing to the East. East Germany is a socialist paradise and it can't afford to absorb the masses of the decadent capitalistic system who are disillusioned with their false high standard of living."

"Yes, Comrade Minister, we got all that in the note. But it's going to sound weak to the neutral countries, particularly since there have been so many pictures of East Germans fleeing to the West but no pictures of West Germans fleeing to the East."

"I'll tell Ulbricht to dress up some of the Volkspolizei in capitalist clothes and you'll have your pictures."

"Thank you, Comrade Minister. Will there be any other stiff notes this week?"

"Just send out the usual form note on disarmament in the regular pouch. There's no sense wasting money on air mail. Have we got any notes on hand threatening Japan this week for its military alliance with the United States?"

"Comrade Sergueivitch wrote a beauty, but because of Comrade Mikoyan's visit we didn't send it out this week."

"What about a stiff note to all the Latin American countries for accepting U.S. financial aid?"

"Comrade Castro asked if he could send it instead. He said it will look stiffer if it's written to them in Spanish."

"All right, but follow it up with a note supporting Castro's note."

"Yes, Comrade. Will that be all?"

"That's all for today. Oh, one more thing. Send a stiff note to the Premier of Finland wishing him a happy birthday."

My Uncle Was Right

WELL, the Communists have been lambasting poor old Stalin and his whole crowd, and it looks like you're going to have to go to Albania if you still want to drive down a street named after him.

The way they talked about Stalin and his friends at the 20th and 21st Congresses would make any counterrevolutionary's hair stand on end. The surprising thing is the party discovered what type of person he was only *after* he died, when so many mistakes had been made.

If they had listened to my Uncle Oscar twenty-five years ago the Russians would have saved themselves a lot of bronze and marble and they might have been building statues to Uncle Oscar now, instead of tearing down ones to Stalin.

I remember as a little boy having dinner one day with my Uncle Oscar in Brooklyn and he said: "That Stalin fellow is a bum."

I had never heard of Stalin before that, and I asked: "What makes you say that, Uncle Oscar?"

"He goes around shooting people and sending them to Siberia and he doesn't do anything for the workers. That fellow is no good, I tell you. He's a troublemaker."

My Uncle Oscar is fairly astute when it comes to politics and so I started following Stalin's career after that. It seemed to me Uncle Oscar had Stalin pegged pretty well, but since my uncle lived in America, it was very difficult to warn the Russians about him.

The next time I heard my Uncle Oscar talk on the subject was when Russia signed a nonaggression pact with Germany and they both attacked Poland. "Stalin is a dirty rat," Uncle Oscar cried. "I hope he drops dead, the miserable stinker. He'd sell his own mother, that louse."

There it was, as clear as day, as far as Uncle Oscar was concerned, but not one person around Stalin, including Nikita S. Khrushchev, saw it that way.

Uncle Oscar was still way ahead of his time.

Russia went to war with Hitler, but Uncle Oscar's opinion of Stalin remained that he was an enemy of the people and a man who couldn't be trusted.

He also at this time developed a dislike for Molotov, Beria, and Vishinsky. "They're all nogoodniks," he shouted at a dinner table one night. "They should have shot them all long ago. If I was in Russia I would pull the trigger myself. First Stalin, then the rest of his lackeys."

"He's killing Germans," my Aunt Molly said. "He can't be all bad."

"Just wait and see what happens after the war. That's when he'll really give us trouble. You mark my words."

How right Uncle Oscar was, and how sad for all of us he wasn't allowed to represent us at Yalta and Potsdam. Not only would Uncle Oscar have refused to divide up Berlin, but he would have been reluctant to let the Russians keep Odessa.

The postwar years for Uncle Oscar were the hardest. He kept sending letters to the Communist Party, warning them about the cult of personality. But they must have considered him some kind of capitalist nut, because they never answered him.

When Stalin ordered the trial of the thirteen doctors for allegedly attempting to poison him, Uncle Oscar lost his temper altogether. "That guy must be crazy."

Sure enough, later events proved Stalin was.

When Malenkov, Beria, and Molotov took over the government after Stalin's death, the first thing Uncle Oscar said was: "They're double-crossing rats, just like Stalin."

Nobody could have been more correct, if we are to believe the minutes of the 20th Communist Congress. Everything Uncle Oscar had said during the last twenty-five years was documented by Khrushchev in spades. What still amazes me is how much he knew about the situation in the Soviet Union before the Communists became aware of it themselves.

Uncle Oscar, on past performance, has never been wrong about the personalities in the Soviet government, so I started to worry the other day when he wrote me a letter and said: "I think this fellow Khrushchev stinks. For my money he's a rat."

I wonder how many more Communist Party congresses will

have to be held before the Russians discover Uncle Oscar
is right again. It kind of scares me to have someone that
clairvoyant right in the family.

Better Fed Than Red

A RECENT issue of the Soviet magazine *Novaya Vremya* (*New
Times*) has been kind enough to devote a page of its valuable
space to an article sympathizing with the difficult job I
have working for a capitalist newspaper. The article points
out that in several pieces I "dared criticize the aggressive
and especially the atomic policy of the Western powers."

"But certain influential quarters in the United States," the
article continues, "did not like that and said so to Buchwald.
He tried to laugh it off and even wrote about the works
he had been given in the United States just because Soviet
periodicals reprinted him.

"Apparently he got his ears boxed for that, for he stopped
meddling in politics and turned to workaday themes and
started writing about French kitchen maids brought home by
rich Americans, what his wife thought of Japanese geishas,
etc., etc.

"The bosses of the *New York Herald Tribune* were not
satisfied with that, and it looks as if they demanded that
Buchwald stop clowning and do something serious. To re-
habilitate himself, poor Art joined the anti-Sovieteers."

The article then goes on to attack a piece I wrote about
the sending of stiff notes by the Soviet Union, and points out
that these stiff notes were aimed at preventing war. The
writer takes pity on me for having to write this kind of stuff,
but indicates it wasn't my fault—I have to pipe another tune
when I work for a newspaper.

How the writer ever found out the background on this I'll
never know. But every word he wrote was true. I can still see
the scene as if it happened yesterday.

I was working on a serious piece proving Russian fallout was really good for people, when my secretary came in to the office, white-faced.

"The bosses want to see you," she said.

When a newspaperman in a capitalist country receives a message like that, he starts shaking uncontrollably.

My secretary cried as I packed a toothbrush, a razor, and the Bible. "Tell my wife she was the best wife a man ever had," I said. And without looking back I went down to the first floor to see the bosses.

They were all there, sailing paper atomic bombs across the room.

"Well, if it isn't 'Better Red Than Dead' Buchwald," the editor sneered. "What took you so long getting down here?"

"Dean Rusk called from Washington and said he didn't like the Soviet Union picking up my articles," I said. "He told me if it doesn't stop, Bobby Kennedy is going to make me ride a freedom bus through Mississippi."

The managing editor, who is a giant of a man, came over and started boxing my ears.

I tried to duck away, but the news editor caught me and *he* started boxing my ears. It was hard to hear much after that.

"We're taking you off politics," the editor said.

"But that's all I know," I cried.

"Well, you're going to start writing about other things or else you'll be in the bread line with the ten million other unemployed. Write about your wife, write about your kids, write about Japanese geishas, but leave our Western warmongering policy alone."

After visiting an ear doctor, I went back to work writing family-type articles. I thought I was doing okay when, in a few weeks, I got another call from the bosses. They wanted to talk to me again. This time I put on a pair of earmuffs before I went in to see them.

"Well, if it isn't 'Better Fed Than Red' Buchwald," the editor sneered. "The Pentagon just called and they're getting sick and tired reading about your wife. They want to know why you haven't joined the anti-Sovieteers."

"No one asked me," I said, trying to duck a blow the managing editor was swinging at me.

"Well, I'm asking you," the editor said. "Now get back to your typewriter and write a violent attack against the Russians, unless you want to join the bread lines with the ten million other unemployed."

"But I don't know anything bad about the Russians," I said. "They're such reasonable, sane, peace-loving people."

The editor nodded to one of his assistants, who gave me a flute. "He'll soon be piping another tune," he said.

I took the flute. "What do you want me to play?"

"Start with 'Yankee Doodle Dandy,'" the editor said, "and we'll tell you how to take it from there."

Is Peace Inevitable?

PEOPLE who have been upset over the way things have been going in the world lately will be happy to know that there is now an organization concerned with peace and its consequences. It's called Ban the Peace, and its major appeal is to people who would like to go to war immediately "and get it over with."

I had the good fortune to talk to the Secretary of BTP and he told me there was more interest in his organization than ever before. "After all the hysterical peacemongering in the United Nations for the past fifteen years," he said, "people are starting to come around to our point of view, that peace is not the answer to the problems facing the world, and some other solution will have to be found. For years we worked alone, just a few dedicated souls stoking the fires of world conflagration, while everyone else sat around talking, talking, talking. But now we're receiving support from almost every corner of the globe, and people are finally becoming frightened of all-out peace."

"But what exactly does your organization do?" I asked the secretary.

Picking up a hand grenade and tossing it up and down, he replied: "Our organization works on the theory that people basically hate each other, and only their leaders are standing in the way of a universal war.

"We try to point out provocations which will lay the groundwork for hostilities. For a short time people were deaf to provocations and would not recognize one if it was thrown in their faces. But things are changing fast. Now people are willing to be provoked on any issue. One of our biggest successes was in Cuba, and the Tunisian crisis showed what you can do with the slightest of provocations. This came as a bonus to us, as we were concentrating all our efforts on Berlin, and we never counted on the French losing their *sang-froid* in North Africa.

"Our organization tries to find intolerable situations such as Kashmir, South Tyrol, and the Congo and we help people work out warlike solutions to problems that otherwise might be solved by peaceful methods. We promote nationalism and encourage people to pay more attention to race, creed, and color. We favor rearmament conferences and military aid to underdeveloped countries.

"We have a package plan called Atoms for War, and we are anxious to get nuclear tests started again. We also have a Missile-to-Missile program, which, when put into effect, will discourage room for negotiation. We believe in getting people into a corner and forcing them to fight their way out."

"This must be a very expensive thing."

"Yes," the secretary said, "but it's not half as expensive as what peace costs. Do you know that people still spend more money on peace than they do preparing for war?"

"It's hard to believe," I said.

"Well, it's true," he said, jabbing a bayonet into his desk. "Look at all these international exchanges, trade fairs, and good-will tours. Just think what you could do with that money if there wasn't a peace? Do you know you could build ten hydrogen bombs for what it costs to build ten universities in Africa? Do you realize you could have constructed an aircraft carrier for the same amount of money that was thrown away on the Olympics last summer? When I think of all the money wasted on technical aid to underdeveloped countries that could have been invested in jet fighters, where it would have done the most good, my blood boils.

"But I shouldn't complain," the secretary said, lighting his cigar with a flame-thrower.

"People are finally beginning to see the light.

"We thought 1956 with Hungary and Suez was the greatest year for Ban the Peace, but this year is shaping up even better. People everywhere are finally getting tired of being *pushed* around!"

The UN Spirit of '76

HAVE you ever wondered what would have happened if there was a United Nations in 1776 when the Americans decided to revolt against George III and the British? It could have been quite interesting.

It was common knowledge in the world at that time that the British were exploiting their American Colonies and the army was behaving badly toward the Americans.

Therefore no one was surprised when the Colonies decided they wanted to revolt. But first they appealed to the United Nations through the Security Council, which consisted of France, England, the Netherlands, Spain, Germany, Portugal, and Russia, to help them get their independence.

A provisional government which included Samuel Adams, Thomas Jefferson, Benjamin Franklin, and John Hancock journeyed to the United Nations to plead their case. But England managed to keep them from appearing in front of the Council by claiming that America was an internal British affair. The provisional government was not representative of the American people, but was in fact a handful of terrorists and radicals who were intimidating the civilian population, according to the English.

England threatened to veto any Security Council resolution concerning her thirteen colonies and warned France, her arch-enemy in the Security Council, that she would not stand interference in what was and always would be a British problem.

The French delegate insisted the Security Council should take up the question of the Colonists immediately. He said he had evidence of British atrocities against the American people, citing the Stamp Act, the Sugar Act, and the Quartering Act as examples of the harsh treatment the British were inflicting on the poor defenseless Americans who had no voice in the government.

The British delegate angrily listed "acts of terrorism" committed by the rebels, including the attacks on British officers and enlisted men in Massachusetts streets, the sabotage of tea in Boston Harbor, and guerrilla raids at Lexington and Concord, where 273 British soldiers were killed "trying to keep the peace."

He cited the vast projects in education, housing, and commerce and the large investments England had made in the new colonies, and he said that "the Americans were not ready to rule themselves at this time" and there would be chaos among the Colonies if Britain did not protect them.

He went on to say that revolutionary attempts were not American-inspired but encouraged by "foreign interests" and that the Americans had been encouraged with money and arms by France and he introduced a resolution asking the Security Council to call on France not to interfere in the American Colonies or it would have to face the consequences.

The consequences, he said, would not rule out the use of Prussian "volunteers" against the American militants.

The French delegate warned that if the British used Prussian volunteers, France was prepared to send French volunteers under the command of General Lafayette to help the freedom-loving Colonists achieve their ends. He said his King was ready to help anyone who wanted to get out from under the yoke of British colonialism, and France would not hesitate to use heavy artillery, the most frightening of all modern weapons, if the British forced them to it.

When a vote on the French resolution to condemn England for her administration in America was taken, the British delegate walked out of the Security Council and said he would not return.

But fearing that the French resolution would be too strong, Portugal and Spain introduced a compromise resolution which would save everyone's face.

Without condemning the British outright, the resolution called on both England and the American Colonies to work out their differences peacefully without interference from any foreign quarter. It urged all its members not to supply guns or troops to the rebel side, and at the same time, it called for the withdrawal of British troops from the Colonies as soon as possible.

The compromise resolution was passed unanimously on July 4, 1776, and thus a revolution in the New World was averted.

The Common Market

THERE is a lot of talk these days about the Common Market and yet people don't seem to understand it. For those who are still confused I'd like to take a try at explaining it.

After World War II Europe was in a mess and so the United States started the Marshall Plan to get it back on its feet. In twelve years Europe got back on its feet and formed the Common Market to put the United States out of business. The United States would now like to make a deal with the Common Market, but some American business groups don't like the idea, because they don't want European goods flooding the American market.

The object of the Common Market is to break down tariffs between the European countries at the same time that they raise them against the outside world.

Europe is split between the Inner Six and the Outer Seven. Great Britain was leader of the Outer Seven, but has asked to become a member of the Inner Six. The only trouble is the British are afraid if they join the Inner Six they'll lose the Commonwealth, which will then turn to the United States for trade. This is one of the reasons the British are suspicious of Jacqueline Kennedy's trip to India and Pakistan.

So the British have one foot in the Inner Six and one foot in the Outer Seven, though the Labour opposition has accused the Tories of putting both feet in their mouths.

The British would like to be in the Common Market and also in the Commonwealth.

But the French don't want them in either. Neither do the Germans. Yet they are considering the British application because the United States asked them to.

In the meantime, the other members of the Outer Seven, excluding Denmark and Norway, want to have the advantages of the Common Market but don't want to join because it will violate their political neutrality. Sweden and Switzerland can't join because their citizens won't let them, and Finland and Austria can't join because Khrushchev won't let them.

Therefore, if Great Britain joins the Inner Six, there won't be any Outer Seven any more. The only thing that can save the neutrals, then, is if Jacqueline Kennedy visits them on her way back from Pakistan.

But the Common Market isn't as strong as it's cracked up to be, because West Germany is hedging on the agricultural part of the treaty. The German farmers are the biggest supporters of Chancellor Adenauer and they are against letting French agricultural products into the country because it might drive down the price of German food, which is government-supported.

France, which still considers itself an agricultural country, insists that unless the Germans drop the tariffs on French food the Common Market treaty has no meaning.

At the same time the French don't like the idea of Danes joining the Common Market because they might drive down the price of French dairy products. But the Danes insist they have to be in the Common Market so they don't lose their trade with West Germany.

The object of the Common Market is to eventually form a United States of Europe with political as well as economic ties. This is one of the reasons the Canadians are against the British joining it.

This more or less sums up the Common Market as it stands today. If anyone has any further questions I suggest they send a penny post card to General de Gaulle.

Great Stories of 1961

THERE were many great stories in 1961. Some made the newspapers—others didn't. These were my favorites of 1961, stories that have never been published before.

It was a cold winter's night in Secret Falls, when Patrolman Sean Morgan was cruising around in his car. Suddenly the radio barked: "Go to 107 Maple Street; a pregnant lady needs help."

Sean turned on his siren and at 80 miles an hour sped to the address. Waiting in front of the house was the nervous husband, who explained his wife was about to have a baby, but he couldn't get his car started and he didn't know what to do.

Sean said he would take the wife in his car, but the husband said it was too late. His wife had started giving birth to the baby in the house.

The patrolman rushed inside and shouted to the husband:

"I want hot water, lots of hot water." The husband dashed into the kitchen and started heating up kettles while Sean went into the bedroom, took off his jacket, and rolled up his sleeves.

In a few minutes the husband dashed in with the boiling water.

Sean smiled sickly and didn't say anything.

"Here's the water," the husband said. "What are you going to do with it?"

"How the hell do I know," Sean said, shrugging his shoulders; "I'm not a doctor."

Charles Weatherspoon hated abstract art and the cult that went with it. When he heard there was going to be an abstract-art exhibition he submitted a painting done by a chimpanzee and then he waited to see the results.

The day of judging arrived, and a group of distinguished art critics walked down the aisles, studying each painting.

Then they came to Weatherspoon's entry. They all stopped and stared and finally the silence was broken by James Corrigan, the greatest abstract-art expert in the United States, who said: "That's the lousiest abstract painted by a chimpanzee that I've ever seen."

Major Roy McMullen, World War II ace, who was shot down in his fighter plane near the end of the war, was stationed in Germany in 1961 as commander of a squadron. One day he was visited by Friedrich von Ralston, a Luftwaffe fighter pilot who had been appointed liaison officer to Major McMullen's outfit.

The two started exchanging war stories and von Ralston told of the day he shot down a P38 over Stuttgart.

"I was shot down over Stuttgart," Major McMullen said, "on November 12, 1944, in a P38."

"That's the day I shot down the plane," von Ralston said excitedly. "It was Number 345."

"Then you shot *me* down," Major McMullen said.

"Yah," von Ralston said. "It was me."

"Why you no good SOB," Major McMullen said, and hit von Ralston right in the teeth.

Mrs. Franklin Wade, the wife of a gamekeeper in Kenya, had raised a lion from babyhood, which she called Eleanor. One day a friend suggested she write a book about her experiences raising the lion. Mrs. Wade was finally persuaded and worked day and night on her book. When it was finished she sent it off to her friend in London, who knew a publisher.

The manuscript was returned to Mrs. Wade in two weeks with a curt note from the publisher. "This is absolutely ridiculous. Everyone knows you can't tame a lion in the jungle."

A Negro Freedom Rider went into an all-white restaurant in Mississippi and sat down at a table. The manager came over immediately and handed him a menu.

"Can I help you, sir?"

The Negro got up immediately and started to leave.

"Is there anything wrong?" the manager asked.

"No," replied the Negro, "except I was so sure you wouldn't serve me, I didn't bring any money."

5.
Is It Safe To Have
a Family?

Dialogue at 30,000 Feet

THE scene is on board Pan American Flight 114 going from New York to Paris. The cast of characters consists of my eight-year-old son and his mother.

My son speaks first: "Mommy, why isn't Daddy talking to you?"

"I don't know why. He's just being silly."

"Mommy, what is overweight?"

"Overweight is when you have more luggage than your ticket allows. It could have happened to anyone."

"What could have happened to anyone?"

"Having overweight. After all, it isn't as if I were carrying back art treasures to Paris. There is nothing in my valises but clothes."

"Are you overweight, Mommy?"

"That awful man at the ticket counter thought I was. I told your father if each of us carried a bag on the plane with us, then that awful man at the counter would not have weighed everything. But your father said we would have been caught."

"What could they have done to us if we had been caught? Maybe they would have taken our luggage away from us?"

"They couldn't do that. I think your father was very foolish allowing them to weigh everything."

"Daddy says for what we paid in overweight we could have all gone first class and still had money left over to send me through Harvard when I grow up."

"He's exaggerating just to make me feel bad."

"He said we could have chartered the *Queen Elizabeth* just for ourselves and gone by ship."

"Don't listen to everything your father tells you."

"He said he told you before we went to the United States that you could only take two bags with you and you took six."

147

"Your father doesn't seem to understand a woman can't travel with just two wash 'n' dry suits."

"Daddy says he doesn't mind you carrying your own clothes but he wants to know why you had to bring back things for every American woman who lives in Paris."

"I didn't bring back clothes for every American woman in Paris. I brought back a coat for Hilda, ski clothes for Marjorie, some shoes for Marion, some girdles for Sophie, and some sweaters for Deborah. Is that every woman in Paris?"

"He said what about the stereo tape recorder for Ursula?"

"That's not clothes."

"And the electric typewriter for Mary-Helen?"

"Now he's hitting below the belt."

"What does that mean?"

"Nothing, it's just an expression. Ask him about the chess set he bought for Jim Nolan."

"He said he sent it by mail."

"I hate righteous people."

"Daddy wants to know if you're going to declare to French customs all the new things you bought for all your friends in Paris?"

"He knows very well I'm not going to."

"He says if you're not would you mind going through customs without him as the French are jailing everyone these days for something or other."

"Everything I bought could very easily belong to me."

"He says he doesn't want anything to do with a smuggler. What is a smuggler?"

"I'm not a smuggler."

"He wants to know what you are."

"I'm a woman, just doing what any normal woman in my position would do."

"He says you're setting a bad example for us."

"Well he's absolutely ridiculous."

"No he's not."

"What do you mean he's not?"

"He just told me what a smuggler was."

How To Enjoy a Gala

I NEVER take my wife to a gala and everyone always asks me why It's quite simple. Take, for instance, La Bal des Petits Lits Blancs, the biggest French charity ball of the year which was held on the new French liner *France*.

The drill was as follows. Thirteen hundred people paying an average of $90 a person left in boat trains at 2:30 Saturday afternoon for Le Havre where the *France* was docked. At 5:30 we were on board where we were given cabins for the night. Then there were tours of the ship, cocktails, a dinner consisting of caviar, foie gras, sole, tournedos, vodka, champagne, Bordeaux, and cognac, all in the splendid French tradition. Then there was a showing of *Breakfast at Tiffany's*, with Audrey Hepburn not only on the screen but appearing in the flesh. This was followed by dancing in three grand salons until seven in the morning. At nine we were given breakfast and at eleven we were all taken back to Paris. It sounds like fun, doesn't it? Well, it was, for some people.

When I arrived at the Gare St. Lazare I met a friend on the platform. He was puffing, struggling with a large white Balmain dress box in one hand and a large jewelry case in the other, and over his arm was a fur stole. His wife was pushing him ahead, urging him to find their compartment before the train left.

"How come you didn't bring your wife?" he asked as he staggered past me.

I shrugged and picked up my one little suitcase and got on the train.

In my compartment on the train going to the ship a Frenchwoman was barking at her husband: "Look at my hair. How can I go to the ball with my hair like this?"

"I took you to the hairdresser this morning," the husband said.

"That was this morning," the wife said bitterly, as I leafed through my latest Agatha Christie.

On board the ship I was shown to my cabin. Fifteen minutes later I ran into a friend in the passageway. He looked white. "My God," he said, "the bath in our stateroom doesn't work and my wife's hysterical. I've got to find the purser or she'll kill herself."

"He's right down the hall," I said.

"Thanks," he said. "By the way, is your wife with you?"

"No," I said, starting a leisurely tour of the boat.

Later on as the dinner hour drew near I heard the desperate cries of men begging stewards to find someone to press their wives' evening dresses at any price, mingled with sobbing of women who couldn't get quite zipped up.

Just before dinner I wandered up to the main deck to see what table I was assigned to for dinner. There was an angry mob of husbands in front of the desk screaming about their table assignments.

I met another friend clawing his way forward.

"They put my wife at one table and me at another," he gasped. "She's fit to be tied. Where are you and your wife sitting?"

"I didn't bring my wife," I said, standing slightly apart from the crowd so I wouldn't get my tuxedo rumpled.

I had a very relaxed dinner watching people arguing with the headwaiters over their table placements.

After dinner there was a fight among the 1,300 people for 664 seats in the movie theater for Miss Hepburn's film. The husbands who didn't make it sat in the bar receiving tongue-lashings from their wives.

When the film was over, the ball began in earnest, and I spent my time dancing with the wives of my friends who weren't speaking to their husbands.

Finally I said, "Well, I guess I'll turn in."

The other men at the table said, "I guess we will too."

But their wives protested. "Not on your life. It's only four o'clock in the morning."

I went back to my cabin and went to sleep, lulled into pleasant dreams by the voices of a couple in the next cabin arguing about the evening.

In the morning on the boat train going back into Paris *no one* asked me why I didn't bring my wife to the ball.

By this time they all knew for themselves.

"One Nice Thing"

EVERY woman likes to own "one nice thing." It may be a dress, it may be a suit, it may be a coat, but it gives her a certain amount of happiness to know she's been extravagant about one item in her wardrobe.

My wife is no different from any other woman in this respect, and last spring she decided to buy her "one nice thing" at Chanel's. It was a cream-colored wool suit with a trim of gold on the jacket pockets and sleeves. She paid somewhere in the neighborhood of three figures for the suit, but she felt it was worth it.

"It was," she said, "the only nice suit I've seen in the collections."

"But for what that suit costs, you could send two Congolese children to school for a year," I protested.

"But I don't know any Congolese children," she said.

She had a point, so I let her keep the suit.

A few weeks later we were dining at the Tour d'Argent when a woman came in wearing the same Chanel suit.

"That lady has the same suit on as you have," I said.

My wife seemed a little annoyed, but all she said was: "I recognize her as a Chanel customer. I suppose she has as much right to the suit as I have."

Several days went by and we were taking tea at the George V. Two women walked in, *both* wearing the suit.

I nudged my wife in a friendly fashion. "Don't look now,

but those two women are wearing your suit. They look to me like twins."

My wife was so angry she refused to eat her chocolate éclair, so I ate it for her.

For a month nothing happened. My wife wore her suit and I almost forgot about what it had cost, when one day I was passing a shop in the Lido Arcade, and there in the window was my wife's suit.

I rushed home to tell my wife the good news .She wouldn't believe me, so I insisted on taking her down to the Lido Arcade to see for herself. Sure enough, there it was in the window and selling for about $90 in francs.

"I think yours is better made," I said, trying to think of something nice to say. But my wife is a very emotional woman and all she kept doing was bite her lips and dab her eyes.

The suit in the Lido Arcade should have been the tip-off for her, but she said: "Maybe the ordinary shop girl won't appreciate the simple design."

How wrong she was! The following week I saw dozens of girls wearing copies of the suit. Some had red fringe, others had black fringe, some were blue, some were green, but the design was the same.

At the end of each day I came home to report to my wife on how many copies of her suit I had seen that day. I thought on the days she didn't get out that she would like to know. But she seemed very surly when I told her, and one time she ran out of the room when I said, "Should I count it as *your* suit if instead of wool it's made of Orlon with Dacron fringe?"

Twelve days later I accidentally saw in a New York paper a full-page ad. Orbach's was having a sale on my wife's suit. I got so excited I called her immediately.

"Guess what?" I said.

"Orbach's is having a sale on my suit," she said.

"How did you know?" I asked, trying to keep the disappointment out of my voice.

"Why else would you call me at two o'clock in the afternoon?" And she hung up.

I guess the last blow came when I was home the other night browsing through a copy of the French *Vogue*. Suddenly I came upon it! A beautiful picture in color of the suit and under it: "We are proud to announce that this suit has been selected as the official uniform of the lady guides at the French Exposition in Moscow."

I tore the page out of the book so my wife wouldn't see it.

It would be too cruel to call her attention to the page now. So I'm saving it to show her on our anniversary next month.

Best-Dressed Woman

HAVE you ever wondered how they select the "Best-Dressed Women of the Year"? Well, apparently they send out ballots to "2,000 style experts and observers of the contemporary fashion scene throughout the world," and we vote. The reason I know all this is that I received a ballot this year asking me to vote for the twelve Best-Dressed Women of 1961, and I must say it was the first time I had been permitted to do anything like this and I hardly knew where to start.

Since the ballot arrived at home, I decided to go no further.

"How would you like to be one of the Best-Dressed Women of 1961?" I asked my wife, who was beating a rug in the back yard.

"How would you like to soak your head in a tub of detergent?" she asked without missing a stroke.

"I'm not kidding," I told her. "Look, here is the ballot. It has a place to list anyone I consider a Best-Dressed Woman. I don't have to sign the ballot, so nobody will know I wrote in your name. They might think Henry Ford II voted for you."

"Who are some of the contestants?" she asked, resting the beater against her sneakers.

"There is a list on the back which they call a reference list. Let's see, there's Marlene Dietrich, Princess Alexandra, the Duchess of Brissac, Mrs. Kirk Douglas, Mrs. Anthony Eden,

Mrs. Nicholas du Pont, Margot Fonteyn, Audrey Hepburn, Mrs. John F. Kennedy, Mrs. Joseph P. Kennedy, Mrs. Claire Boothe Luce, Princess Margaret, Princess Radziwill, Queen Sirikit of Thailand, and Mrs. Stavros Niarchos, among others. Do any of these present serious competition?"

"None that I can see," she said, untying the red bandana on her head. "It looks like I've got the thing sewed up."

"You don't have to worry about Claudette Colbert, the Duchess of Windsor, Queen Elizabeth II, Princess Grace, Mrs. William Randolph Hearst, Jr., Mrs. William Paley, or Madame Arturo Lopez-Willshaw," I told her.

"Why, do they make their own clothes?"

"No, because they're lifetime members of the Hall of Fame. They could wear overalls and nobody could say they're not well dressed. They're so well dressed we're forbidden to vote for them."

"That narrows down the competition, then, doesn't it?" she said, taking off her rubber gloves. "You take those girls out of the race and it's everyone for herself."

"Exactly my feelings," I told her. "How do you think you could do against Rosalind Russell?"

"Furs or evening clothes?" she asked.

"You're the challenger, you have the choice of weapons."

"Then I'll take raincoats. I have three."

"Suppose you and Mrs. Benson Ford walked into the same party. Do you think you could take her?"

"In a fair fight with just cocktail dresses and pearl necklaces?" she asked.

"Yes."

"The answer is no," she said. "Not even if the Ford Company goes into its worst slump in years."

"If you're going to be one of the Best-Dressed Women you can't have that defeatist attitude," I said. "It isn't what you wear, it's the way you wear it.

"Let me put it this way. You're at a ball in Washington. Mrs. John Kennedy, Mrs. Joseph Kennedy, and Mrs. Robert Kennedy come in. What would you do?"

"I'd look for President Kennedy. He couldn't be very far behind."

"No, no, no. The point is, why would you feel that they were better dressed than you were?"

"Because they weren't beating rugs all day, for one thing."

"Well, I'm going to vote for you anyway. We have nothing to lose."

"And," she said, "suppose I win?"

The Morning After

It was nine-thirty on New Year's morning when I first heard the frightening noise. It sounded like ten thousand Baluba tribesmen trying to get into my bedroom.

Things were too blurred to see, but the din became closer and finally the Balubas crashed into the bedroom wearing paper hats, blowing horns, hitting drums, and sounding whistles.

"What the hell are you doing with those noisemakers?" I croaked to three of the tribesmen, who were starting to look like my children.

"We found them in the hall by your overcoats," my eight-year-old son said. "Look, Daddy, if you blow on this balloon it makes noise when the air is let out."

"I know all about that balloon," I said, holding my ears. "Now put those damn things away."

"Well, why did you bring them home then, if we can't play with them?" my seven-year-old daughter asked as she twirled a stick that sounded like a 20-millimeter cannon.

"I didn't bring them home," I cried. "Your mother brought them home. Her last words to me were: 'We have to bring home one of everything for the children.'"

"Make them go away," my wife groaned from under the pillow she was holding over her head.

"Now you can say that. This morning at three there weren't

enough noisemakers in Maxim's for *your* children. You made me tip the waiter to get two extra drums."

My six-year-old started playing a toy saxophone.

"Please, kids," I begged. "It's New Year's morning. Isn't there anything sacred in your lives?"

My eight-year-old son stopped playing a harmonica. "Daddy, what are all these things for?"

"What do you mean, what are they for?"

"Well, why do people have them?" he asked.

"To make noise with," I said.

"Well," he said brightly, "that's what we're doing with them. What's wrong with that?"

I tried to get a good grip on the sides of the bed. "You're only supposed to make noise with them at midnight on New Year's Eve."

"But we're not allowed to stay up to midnight on New Year's Eve, so why can't we play with them now?"

"Because nobody is supposed to make noise on New Year's Day. It's written in the Koran!" I yelled.

"If you're going to shout," my wife said from under her pillow, "you can leave, too."

"But Daddy," my son persisted, "why do people make noise on New Year's Eve?"

"Because they're celebrating."

"Celebrating what?"

"They're celebrating that one year is over and a new year is beginning."

"Why?"

"Just because that's what people do. They don't even know why they do it themselves. It's really silly, if you ask me."

"Then why do *you* do it?"

"Because it doesn't seem silly at the time. At the time it seems the thing to do."

"Well," my son said, persisting in his logic, "why can't we celebrate New Year's now?"

"Because your mother and I were celebrating it last night, that's why."

"I don't know which is worse," my wife mumbled, "the noisemakers or your explanations."

"Why don't you go in the kitchen and celebrate New Year's with Danielle [our cook]?" I said.

"She won't let us," my six-year-old daughter said.

"Well, why don't you go down in the courtyard and celebrate it with the concierge?"

"He won't let us," my seven-year-old daughter said.

"Well, suppose we celebrate late this afternoon?" I suggested.

"We can't because Lancelot is on television," my son said, "and if we made any noise we couldn't hear it."

A Terrible Dilemma

EVERYONE admires people who can afford servants, but they have problems, like everybody else, and some of them are caused by the fact that they can afford servants in the first place. Yesterday I was visited by an old and dear friend who was very upset and wanted to talk to me.

"Jane [his wife] and the cook are fighting," he told me. "And I'm in the middle. Jane says that if the cook Marguerita, doesn't go, she's leaving, and Marguerita says if Jane doesn't go, she's leaving. I'm facing a terrible choice."

"You really are in a mess," I agreed. "Isn't there any chance of getting them together?"

"I doubt it," my friend said. "They've been quarreling for months, petty things, but the writing is on the wall. Thanksgiving was the final blow. Jane tried to tell Marguerita how to cook the turkey. Marguerita said she knew how to cook a turkey. Jane said she wanted to cook the turkey the American way, with bread and sage stuffing. Marguerita said that was a ridiculous way to cook a turkey, almost as ridiculous as serving cranberry sauce with the bird. Everyone in France knows you serve turkey with chestnut dressing and currant jelly.

"Jane finally came in and said that since I had spoiled Marguerita to the point where she wouldn't listen to anyone else anyway, would I tell her to make the turkey with bread stuffing. But I made the mistake of saying I didn't mind *my* turkey with chestnut stuffing."

"As far as I see it, old boy, the choice is quite simple—you either keep your wife or you keep the cook," I said. "Which is it going to be?"

"That's the trouble," he said. "I can't make up my mind. It isn't hard to find another wife, but good cooks are getting damned scarce.

"Jane may know how to cook a turkey, but that's all she knows how to cook, and if I back my wife against the cook, she's sure to leave. After all, Thanksgiving comes only once a year and how many times can you eat turkey?"

"You've got a point," I admitted. "Let's probe a little deeper. Do you love your wife?"

"Of course I love my wife," he said angrily. "What a silly question to ask."

"Do you love the cook?"

"Of course not," he said. "But I do love what she cooks. No one can make a lobster soufflé the way she does. And her *quenelles au chablis* is better than anything you can find in Paris. You can't believe what she can do with a *poularde normande*. Some nights when I am tired and say I'm not very hungry she makes me a little omelette *basquaise*. And she knows I don't like roquefort in my salad dressing. It would be just my luck if I let her go and then found someone who put roquefort in my salad. What would you do in my situation?"

"It's hard to say," I replied honestly. "I hope I'll never have to make the decision, particularly for the children's sake. Does your wife have any qualities comparable to those of your cook?"

"She's a wife. What else can I say about her? Everybody's got a wife."

"Couldn't you fix it so Jane doesn't go into the kitchen and Marguerita doesn't come into the living room?"

"No," he said. "Jane's a wonderful girl, but she's got this stupid idea that she should be able to tell the cook what to do. Do you know, she actually accused me of disloyalty because I sided with the cook over a silly argument concerning a mousse *au chocolat*. Would you say I was disloyal?"

"Certainly not," I said. "You would have been disloyal to your cook if you had sided with your wife."

"That's what I thought," he said, very much relieved. "But that still doesn't solve the problem."

"Why don't you leave it like this. Ask your wife to make more of an effort, try to impress on her that, as much as you feel about her, there is more in life than just love. If she still won't co-operate I don't see where you have a choice."

"You mean divorce?" he said.

"I can't see any other way out. Can you?"

"No," he said. "I wish there was another solution, but I'll be darned if either one of us can think of it."

The Cook in the Attic

A FRIEND of mine, a lady who lives in Switzerland, had a cook who had been working in the family for fifty years, first with her late husband's family and then for her. Anna was very fond of the lady's husband, but never cared too much for the lady herself.

This year Anna seemed to be having hallucinations. At first she reported my friend to the police for waiting until Anna went to bed and then sending up noise through the radiator in the cook's room so she couldn't sleep.

The police didn't pay any attention to this, so Anna got very mad and wrote a letter to the police saying that my friend was poisoning college students who were invited to the house for lunch and then the bodies were put in trunks in the attic. Anna estimated that twenty college students had been done away with by her boss, who was the only one who had the key to the attic.

Anna signed this letter and the Préfet de Police came to the house to have tea with my friend.

The Préfet produced the letter from Anna and my friend became furious and took the Préfet up to the attic to prove that there were no bodies there. The Préfet assured my friend he knew this to be so, but he had to check it anyway. He went away happy that the matter was closed.

My friend then went to Anna and said: "This has to stop. You shouldn't have sent a letter like that to the police."

Anna did not deny sending the letter. All she said was: "It could have been true."

The next day my friend had three friends in for lunch, and as they sat down Anna brought out the first course, which consisted of a creamed veal dish. My friend didn't say anything.

The next dish was brought out, which turned out to be beef Stroganoff. The third course was fried veal cutlets, and for dessert Anna served frankfurters with sauerkraut.

My friend was absolutely in tears. Accusing her of murder was one thing, but serving a lunch like that was unforgivable, so she decided to take Anna down to the police station and make a complaint.

She told Anna to get into the car. My friend was terribly excited as she drove toward the police station, so much so that she didn't see a dog crossing the street and killed him.

The man who owned the dog came rushing out of the house and screamed: "You killed my dog."

My friend said: "It was an accident. I didn't see the dog."

Then Anna got into the act and said: "It's not true. She did it purposely. She has already killed twenty college students and put their bodies in the attic."

The man said: "Well, let's go to the police."

My friend said: "That's where I was going anyway."

Now all three were going to the police station, each for a different reason.

When they arrived they all started talking at once.

The man complained my friend killed his dog. Anna complained my friend killed the college students, but the weakest complaint of all was my friend's, who tried to explain what Anna had served for lunch.

To make matters worse, my friend said: "My mother always told me to take servants at the age of sixteen and beat them once a week for two years and at the age of twenty they'll be excellent servants."

An eager young Swiss policeman immediately took out his notebook and said: "What is your mother's name?"

The outcome of my friend's visit to the police station was that Anna offered to be a witness for the man when he made his complaint about his dead dog.

But no one was interested in my friend's complaint. Apparently there is no law in Switzerland forbidding a cook from serving four meat courses in a row.

House for Rending

A FRIEND of mine rented his house on the Long Island shore for the summer while he was traveling abroad with his family. Then he remembered he had forgotten to tell the man he had rented the house to that someone was coming to fix the oil burner, which was in a locked room in the cellar. So he decided to call his house and tell the man where the workers could find the key. He said the conversation went something like this.

"Hello, this is Mr. Mellon," my friend said. "I just wanted to . . ."

"Oh hello Mr. Mellon," the wife of the man who rented the house said. "My husband isn't home now."

"That's all right," Mr. Mellon said. "How is everything?"

"Just fine, Mr. Mellon. We're really enjoying the house—Peter, will you stop pulling on those curtains, I'm talking on the phone. The children love it here— Wanda, what are you doing with those scissors . . . Peter, take those scissors away from Wanda. . . . Excuse me, Mr. Mellon, it's raining out and the children have to stay indoors. What did you call about, Mr. Mellon? . . . One minute, Peter, put those scissors down and get away from the drapes. . . . Ethel, you know you're not supposed to eat ice cream in the living room. Now will you all be quiet. Go ahead, Mr. Mellon."

"I called to tell you that some men are going to come to fix the oil heater and I wanted you to know it was all right to let them in and to tell you where the key was for the cellar."

"Why certainly Mr. Mellon. . . . Wanda get down off that coffee table this instant. I don't care what Peter did this morning, you're not supposed to climb on Mr. Mellon's coffee table. . . . Peter, take Wanda into the kitchen while I'm talking on the phone. . . . No, don't use the scissors, just take her by the hand. . . . I'm still here, Mr. Mellon."

Mr. Mellon was perspiring.

"Now what did you say, Mr. Mellon?"

"The key for the oil burner—"

"Can you hold on one minute, Mr. Mellon? . . . Ethel, get away from the lamp. How many do you have to break before you learn your lesson? . . . Peter, I told you to take Wanda into the kitchen. . . . Tell her I'll give her a good spanking if she plays with Mr. Mellon's dishes. She knows we're not allowed to use *those* dishes. . . . I'm sorry, Mr. Mellon, but it's the third day it's been raining and the children are wild."

"Where's your husband?" Mr. Mellon asked.

"He went down to buy some rosebushes to replace the ones in your garden."

"What was the matter with *my* rosebushes?" Mr. Mellon demanded.

"Nothing, except the children were playing with the dog and he got excited and. . . . Ethel, I've told you you can't paint on Mr. Mellon's desk. Go in the kitchen with Peter and

Wanda and find out what that crash was. . . . But don't worry, Mr. Mellon, my husband saved the irises and begonias. Hello, Mr. Mellon, are you there?"

"Almost," Mr. Mellon said weakly.

"You were saying about the key for the oil burner?"

"It's in the laundry closet hanging on a nail."

"Oh, that's what the key was for. Peter found it the first day and we had no idea what it was for. Peter! Peter, what did you do with that key . . . you know the one you had the first day. . . . Well think, Peter; it's very important. . . . You couldn't have traded it for a whistle. . . . Well you just tell Waldo you want the key back. . . . Don't worry, Mr. Mellon, we'll find it.

"I'm sure my husband will be terribly disappointed he wasn't here to talk to you himself, but I know he'd want me to thank you for renting us the house for the summer, and tell you what a blessing it's been. It was terribly thoughtful of you to call."

There was a crash and then silence.

Mr. Mellon doesn't seem to be enjoying Europe as much as Mrs. Mellon thought he would and he hasn't the heart to tell her why.

6.
Is It Safe To Live
in Paris?

Good Will to All

BESIDES everything else President de Gaulle has to think about, he is constantly having heads of state drop in on him for so-called good-will visits. There was a time a few years ago when it took the Queen of England, the President of the United States, or the Premier of Russia before the French would decorate the city of Paris with flags and give the visitors the full treatment. But now it doesn't make any difference *who* comes to Paris—if you're the head of state, any state, you get the works, which means flags on the Champs Elysées, dinner with General de Gaulle, a ride up to the Arc de Triomphe with all traffic at a halt, a 21-gun salute, and a special performance at the Opéra or Comédie Française.

Not only are these trips costly, but they're getting on the nerves of the French, whose good will has always been at a minimum anyway.

Take the visit of the Shah of Iran. Before the Shah came to Paris on a good-will visit, the French, if they thought about him at all, believed he was a nice chap, good-looking, obviously rich, and a good picker of beautiful wives. They knew his present wife shopped at Christian Dior, which always means a lot to a Frenchman, and that his former wife couldn't produce a male heir, which always makes a Frenchman very sad.

Therefore I could say the Shah of Iran had a certain amount of good will among the Parisians *before* he came.

But then he arrived, the flags went up, the Garde Républicaine turned out, the cannon were shot off, and there were traffic jams all over the city.

Taxi drivers used the name of the Shah in vain, husbands who couldn't get home to their *cassoulet* turned against Iran overnight, people on Paris buses started to discuss how to overthrow the Persian throne. In just three days every bit of good will was used up, and it will be a long time between good-will visits before the French will forgive the Shah for coming to Paris.

Almost every week a president of a new African republic shows up in Paris and the scene is repeated.

The countries are so new that sometimes the flags are flown upside down. Other times they're flown sideways. No one seems to notice until the African president takes his drive up the Champs Elysées. Then he's horrified, insulted, and the French have to give him even more money than he asked for to make up for the mistake.

What can be done to make good-will visits a matter of good will again? Raymond Loewy, the industrial designer, has been studying the problem and he thinks he has come up with some ideas.

First, he thinks, the French could save money on the cost of the flags by having zippers on the different colors. Then instead of making new flags for each state visit, the colors could be zipped together to correspond with the colors of the flag.

If this is too expensive, he suggests the French build billboards along the main thoroughfares and project the flags on the billboards with a slide projector.

As to the traffic snarls caused by state visits, Mr. Loewy comes up with this suggestion:

The French should refurbish a Métro car with Louis XIV furniture, a bar, a salon and, if need be, a bedroom. Then the head of state could go from one function to another on the subway, which is not only faster but much safer from a *plastique* point of view. So the visitor won't be unhappy, they could pipe in over a loud-speaker the sounds of the cheering throngs, with an occasional "Vive Président Thatsabubu" rising above the noise of the crowd.

As a farewell gift, President de Gaulle can give the head of state a set of 8-mm. movies of the places in Paris he didn't get to see, to look at when he gets back home.

The Sirens of Paris

MANY American friends have asked me if the French are as nervous about a Russian attack as they are. No one here is talking about fallout shelters, nor has there been any interest in the manufacture or sale of survival kits. There is in fact no interest in civil defense at all.

For example, the other day the air raid sirens in Paris sounded at 11:30 in the morning. The sirens are always tested on the first Thursday of every month at noon, so when they went off at 11:30 I naturally became a little apprehensive, not only because the Russians might attack Paris, but the French Army could attack as well.

I rushed down into the street to see what was going on. Nothing was going on.

"Did you hear the sirens go off?" I asked the doorman of the California Hotel.

"Yes," he said.

"Why do you think they went off at eleven-thirty instead of noon?"

"It's probably got something to do with the opening of the Auto Show."

I went next door to an art gallery. "Did you hear the sirens go off?"

"Yes," the gallery owner said. "In this traffic I wish I had a siren on my car. I would show them."

At the Berri Bar I asked a group of workers drinking their morning ration of wine if they had heard the sirens go off. Some had.

"Why do you think they were sounding?" I asked a truck driver.

He shrugged his shoulders. "C'est la guerre."

I decided the only thing to do was go back to the office and call up the French government officials. Surely if something was wrong they would know.

The first bureau I called was the Police Commissariat of the Champs Elysées district. An official denied hearing any sirens. I told him I was very frightened. He said he was very sorry and he would send in a report on it. His advice to me was to call the central police station of the 8th Arrondissement.

I called the station. A man answered, and when I asked him why the siren had sounded he said he hadn't heard it. "Has anyone besides you heard it?" I became very indignant. "Everyone heard it," I shouted. He said: "Call the Préfecture of the Seine. In the meantime we will send in a report on it."

I called the Préfecture of the Seine, which gave me the Directeur du Service Technique. He said: "We are not responsible for sirens, but since you called I will make a report on it. There is a Service Technique des Sirènes which is in charge of this, but you are not allowed to call them. You must call the Cabinet du Préfet to get authorization to call the Service Technique des Sirènes."

I was switched over to the Cabinet du Préfet where, after speaking to two people, I was turned over to someone who asked me again: "Has anyone else besides you heard it?" I started twitching. "Yes," I said. "The doorman of the California Hotel heard it. I might be a liar, but the concierge will swear for him." He then said: "This is very serious. The first Thursday in September it went off at five past twelve. There must be something wrong. We are not responsible. You must call the Service de la Protection Civile."

I dialed the civil defense bureau and the woman who answered was embarrassed.

"We are not responsible for the sounding of the siren, monsieur," she said in a hurt voice. "We are only responsible for the distribution of the sirens around town. The button is not in this office."

"Who should I call?" I said.

"Call the Service Technique of the Préfet de la Seine."

"I already called there," I said. "They told me to call you.

All I want to know is, are the Russians attacking France or aren't they?"

"Why don't you call the American Embassy?" she suggested.

I was just about to give up when I saw in the phone book a telephone number for the Service des Sirènes.

I called the number but there was no answer.

Four Men in the Métro

WHILE I was in Rome there was an electricity strike in Paris which affected everything, including the Métro. The Métro trains had enough power to move along for about six hundred feet, then stop and then move again, and it took my secretary Ursula and a Swiss friend of hers about two hours to get to their destination.

But it wasn't a wasted trip as she reported to us.

They were talking Swiss Deutsch, Ursula told me, and just behind their seats stood two elderly Frenchmen, one with a Legion of Honor in his buttonhole, the other wearing an old-fashioned pince-nez. They listened to Ursula's conversation for a while without understanding a word, and then the train stopped in the middle of the tunnel.

The man with the Legion of Honor said: "Isn't it sad about all these strikes? Just think of all those poor foreigners who are here on vacation. What an impression they must get of France!"

His friend nodded his head sadly, as did two younger men who stood nearby. The old man continued: "I say no country is a great country as long as its subways don't work properly." They all nodded again.

One of the young men said: "I think it's disgusting about all these strikes. The foreigners will go home and tell everyone about it and our reputation will be terrible. I tell you what the French should do. They should give every foreigner who leaves France after a strike a present—so they won't tell anyone. Let's give the women a bottle of perfume and the men a bottle of cognac. Then they would go home and say France is a great country."

The old man with the pince-ez looked shocked: "Monsieur, that would be bribery."

His friend with the Legion of Honor agreed: "No country is really great as long as it has to bribe people into talking nicely about it."

The young Frenchman had a disgusted look on his face. "Why don't they give those poor electricity workers a raise? All branches which have any contact with foreigners, like the Métro, the railway, the buses, the planes, electricity, gas, and water should never be allowed to strike. Why don't they cut the salaries of people who work where foreigners never go— like the Ministry of War Veterans?"

The man with the Legion of Honor became angry: "Ah! Monsieur, what nonsense! I am a war veteran, and let me tell you no country is really great unless it treats its war veterans well."

There was another silence. Then the man with the Legion of Honor started chuckling—he seemed to have a good idea. "I think we should make sacrifices for foreigners so they will have an excellent impression of France. On days of transportation strikes, we should all leave our cars in the street with big signs on them saying, 'Help yourself to my car—just return it tomorrow.'"

His friend with the pince-nez chuckled. "Very good, very good. Just think of what glorious reports of France all foreigners would take home with them."

One of the young men shouted disagreement. "Oh no, oh no. I have yet to meet a foreigner who drives decently. None of them knows how to treat a car, none. I hate to think what would happen to my Quatre Chevaux in the hands of these brutes who drive those American monsters. Perhaps if we did this, foreigners would think we were a great country, but I certainly wouldn't."

The man with the Legion of Honor chuckled. "You wouldn't think that way if you didn't own a car."

Twenty minutes later the men were still talking. The old man with the pince-nez said: "If we have fewer tourists in France than other years it's because of all the strikes. No one is sure when they can leave the country or how."

The young man said: "I don't think it's because of the strikes people aren't coming—it's because of the bombs. That's what's frightening people off."

"No," said the man with the pince-nez. "I have a cousin in America who wrote to me he was planning to come to Paris, but he decided, because of the danger, he was going to Russia instead. If he's going to Russia he obviously isn't afraid of bombs, but of the strikes in France. The Russians have lots of bombs, but no strikes. That's why they're getting all the tourists."

Health Is Everything

A DOCTOR's life in Paris can be a very interesting one, particularly when he is called upon to treat visiting tourists.

Recently a doctor friend of mine was called in the late afternoon to a hotel by a woman who said she thought her husband was having a heart attack.

When he arrived the wife was hysterical, and while the doctor was examining the patient the wife kept berating her husband.

"I told you you shouldn't work so hard. How many times have I told you to slow down? You think you're a young man, but you're not any more, and this should be a lesson to you. Business, business, business, that's all you ever think of. But you've never thought of me. What good is all your business if things like this are going to happen? Doctor, is he going to be all right?"

"Well," the doctor said, "all this talking isn't helping him much, nor is all this shouting and hysteria. We're going to have to take a cardiogram."

"A cardiogram!" the wife screamed at her husband. "How many times have I told you to take it easy? How many times have I said you'd wind up like all your friends who worked all the time? But you wouldn't listen. No, you were too smart. Now you have to take a cardiogram."

"Madam," the doctor said patiently, "there is nothing wrong with taking a cardiogram. I don't think there is anything wrong with your husband but I just want to make sure. Now please try to be quiet and let your husband rest until I can get a specialist to come over with the equipment."

"That's easy for you to say," the wife cried, "but you've never seen him work. Day and night that's all he ever thinks about—his business. How many times I have said: 'Keep it up, just keep it up, make a widow out of me. Then see what good your sales charts are to you.'

"Did he listen to me? He did not. Now look at him stretched out there on the bed. Doctor, money is no object, just get him better, that's all I ask."

The doctor said: "Madam, I told you I don't think there is anything wrong with your husband. He just looks to me as if he's very tired and needs some rest. Apparently he's been going at a terrible pace."

"You can say that again," the wife said. "I told him to slow down, I . . ."

The doctor went into the other room and called a cardiogram specialist.

Two hours later the specialist arrived with his nurse and the doctor returned to see the results.

The cardiogram showed that there was nothing wrong with the husband.

The wife was tremendously relieved. "It's like having a gift from heaven," she said. "We can even go to the Lido tonight."

"I'm a little tired," the husband said weakly.

"You're tired," the wife said angrily. "What about me after what I've been through today? You're always thinking of yourself. I'm twice as tired as you, but I didn't come to Europe to spend time in a hotel room. It's your first vacation in years and you don't even want to go out and do anything. We could have stayed at home for all the fun we're having. I knew we shouldn't have come. You don't know how to enjoy yourself. 'I'm tired,' that's all I ever hear from you."

The doctor tried to help the husband. "I do think your husband should take it easy for a week or so. Why don't you go to Switzerland and rest for ten days or so?"

"I didn't come to Europe to rest in Switzerland," the wife replied. "I suppose that's your idea of a good time?"

Then the wife said: "All right, we won't go to the Lido tonight, but we're still going to the Louvre tomorrow. No French doctor is going to spoil *our* vacation."

A Taxing Afternoon

As a student of French bureaucracy, I am constantly amazed at the twists and turns it takes and how difficult it is to win even a minor skirmish in the great "Red Tape of Courage." Some time ago, I was informed by a division of the French tax authority that I was violating Napoleonic Code No. bla-bla-bla because I was paying taxes to one bureau, when in fact I should have been paying these taxes to another.

I wrote back immediately saying I was sorry I was paying taxes to the wrong division, but since that bureau had accepted the money, and I assumed it all went into the same kitty, I was in the clear. But if I was doing something wrong, I assured them I would be most happy to rectify the mistake. I asked them what I should do.

In discussing the matter with my French lawyer later, I realized I had made a great error in replying to *their* letter. "You fool," he berated me. "Now they'll really have it in for you. They don't expect anyone to reply to the first letter they send out—they count on at least three or four warnings before they expect to hear from you."

"What's the difference?"

"The difference is that if everyone replied immediately to a summons from the tax department they would be deluged with work and unable to do a decent job. They had a second letter ready to go out to you, taking you to task for not answering the first one. But since you have answered the first one, you threw a wrench into the entire machinery. I'll call them and tell them you're a foreigner and that you take government letters too seriously. Perhaps they'll be lenient."

A few weeks later I received another letter informing me an inspector was coming to see me and wanted a time set aside for an interview.

I gave the Inspector an appointment and waited nervously for him to appear. He finally arrived with a large briefcase stuffed with forms. He was very friendly as he sat down in a chair. He had a long speech prepared explaining that he didn't like bothering me any more than I liked being bothered, but the law was the law and the state was the state.

I cut him short. "You're perfectly right," I said. "How much do I owe you?"

Shock and then disappointment registered on his face.

"Aren't you going to protest?" he said.

"No, sir. I want to pay what you think I owe."

"But, but . . ." he said, horrified. "All journalists protest to us. They believe the law in regard to them is unfair."

"That's their business," I said. "I think the law is fair. I don't even know what the law is, but I'm not going to fight it."

"But if you fight it and we give you an adverse ruling, you can appeal it to the commission, and after the commission you can go to the court, and after the court you might even have the matter raised in Parliament."

"No, thank you. I don't want to wind up in a French court."

"But you don't understand. Your position is even better. You're an American living in France. By the time it got to court you might not even be here any more. Why don't you protest like everybody else and stop making trouble?"

"I'm sorry. I insist on paying."

Wearily, the Inspector took out his forms. "All right," he said. "Where was your wife born?"

"What's that got to do with it?" I asked.

"Are you protesting?" he asked hopefully.

"No! She was born in Pennsylvania," I shouted.

In an hour he had everything written down. Sadly he got up to leave.

"We will let you know what you owe us. Frankly, monsieur, I am very disappointed. I saw this as a six-month job. The foreign complication in itself would have taken up three months of it. If you had protested, it would have gone on up and up to the highest level. We wouldn't have received a ruling for maybe a year—a year and a half."

"I'm sorry," I told him honestly.

"The only thing I don't understand," he said, "is why, if you weren't going to protest, you answered our letter in the first place."

Auto Polo Meeting

THE Auto Polo Club of France held its annual meeting in the middle of the Place de la Concorde Monday with Milton H. Wallach, founder and president of the APC of F in the chair (it was actually a stretcher).

Rounding up members for the meeting was a formidable task. There were plenty of arms and legs, but Mr. Wallach had difficulty finding heads that went with them.

Many of the French Auto Polo players have turned professional and become taxi drivers. This was discovered by Mr. Wallach when he got into a taxi and looked at the meter.

"Your clock is ticking," Wallach complained.

To which the cabby replied: "You aren't riding on four wheels yourself."

The meeting took up some of the important questions of the sport which is now being played in every part of France except where the farmers have blocked the roads with tractors. As everyone knows, the object of Auto Polo is for the player, seated behind the wheel of his car, to drive a pedestrian through a predetermined goal post without doing any harm to his own vehicle.

Defensively, the second object of the game is to prevent another car from scoring by pinning the pedestrian down until the policeman blows his whistle.

The question of plastic bumpers came up at the meeting, and a member asked that they be outlawed because they gave too much bounce to the pedestrians and were causing far more goals to be scored than the old chrome bumpers of previous years.

He said that all the fun was going out of the game by making it too easy to drive pedestrians up into the air.

The rules committee adopted some new proposals to help the game. Anyone going through a stop sign at less than 50 miles per hour will have his tires automatically deflated for ten days. Leaving the scene of an accident without boasting about it will lead to immediate suspension.

A resolution was also passed complaining about the large insurance awards given to victims of Auto Polo accidents in France. The Auto Polo Club complained officially that these awards, handed down by juries many of whom have never even participated in the sport, were hurting the game.

"We don't expect to make money at Auto Polo," the owner of a custom-built Facel-Vega complained. "At the same time, we don't want to lose any."

Another resolution was passed taking General de Gaulle to task for closing off the Champs Elysées (the Yankee Stadium of Auto Polo) to traffic during the recent visit of President Kennedy and his wife Jacqueline.

The Auto Polo Club requested that on future visits heads of

state use side streets when driving up to the Arc de Triomphe, as they did in the case of the President of Germany, Luebke, when he was a guest of France.

The Auto Polo Club also complained of the lack of American tourists on the Champs Elysées this year. American tourist pedestrians always made the best pucks for Auto Polo, but with the lack of Americans players they have had to use German, Belgian, and Dutch pedestrians in their place. These pucks are much heavier and some have done damage to the players' headlights.

A research committee was formed to see if a substitute could be found for a lightweight American tourist.

The meeting broke up in confusion when a member complained that Paris streetwalkers were now driving sports cars in the Champs Elysées area and were interfering with the game because they were far more interested in picking up pedestrians than knocking them down.

Playing GAD in Paris

GOING to large receptions and cocktail parties can be fun, particularly if you play the game. The game is called "Getting a Drink" or, for short, GAD, and can be played by any number of people on any kind of reception floor.

The other night I played a wonderful match at the wedding reception of a dear friend of mine. The house where the reception was given was jammed with people and the bar was located at the farthest end of the room, ideal conditions for the sport.

I started from the goal line, or, if you will, the reception line. The first person I met was the wife of a dear friend of mine whose name I couldn't remember.

"How are you?" she asked.

"I'm fine, thank you," I replied. "Can I get you a drink?"

"Yes, thank you. I'm drinking a vodka martini."

I butted my head into the crowd and made three yards. At this point I was grabbed by the arm and held by a dear friend who works in the embassy whose name I couldn't remember.

"Staying in town for the holidays?" he said, holding me firmly.

"Yes, are you?" I said trying to get my arm free.

"No, we're going away."

"That's nice. Can I get you a drink?"

"Why not?" he said, letting me go. "I'm drinking Scotch on the rocks."

I broke away and this time decided on an end-run. I was almost in the clear when I was blocked by a large society woman whose name I couldn't remember.

"You naughty boy," she said, throwing me for a loss. "You never write about my charity."

"I plan to next week," I said. "Can I get you a drink?"

"How sweet of you. I'm drinking champagne."

"Champagne," I repeated, running off tackle straight into a huddle.

The huddle was composed of four men who were arguing about Roger Maris's sixty-first home run.

"Here's someone who can tell us," one of them, whose name I couldn't remember, said.

"What game did Roger Maris hit his sixty-first home run in and what team was he playing against?" was the question.

"I don't know," I said quite honestly, but then, noticing the disappointment on their faces, I asked: "Can I get refills for you gentlemen?"

"I'm drinking a martini," said one.

"Make mine an old-fashioned with sugar."

"Straight Irish whisky for me."

"Gin and bitters, thank you."

I broke away from the huddle, feinted as if I was going to pass, but instead found a hole between an Old Guard and her linebacker. Before anyone could stop me I had made seven, then eight, then nine yards and was finally brought down twelve yards from the goal by my family doctor, whose name I couldn't remember.

"How's the liver?" he asked.

"Getting better," I said. "Can I get you a drink?"

"I'll have a baby Scotch, but you better not have anything."

"Exactly what I've been thinking," I said, and then dove past him straight-arming a French marquis and throwing a hefty block at an Italian countess, who was all set to trip me.

I was stopped short at the goal by the best man whose name I couldn't remember.

"Pretty crowded," he said.

"Quite," I replied, not taking my eye off the kitchen door behind the bar which led into the street.

"Here comes the bride," I said. As he looked around I ducked under the table, dashed for the kitchen door, and made it out into the street for a touchdown.

If I must say so myself, it was one of the greatest GAD games I have ever played.

Twistin' on the Floor

THE TWIST with all its ramifications has hit Paris in a big way. Night clubs that were dying have been saved by the craze, students who were planning riots have postponed them in favor of the dance, the great cultural vacuum in France has been filled by American rock 'n' roll favorites, and, for the moment, the town doesn't know whether to twist or overthrow the government.

I don't know how they do the Twist in America, but in France it's something to watch. It isn't just the gyrations of everyone's rear axle that makes the Twist such an interesting spectator sport, but what goes on behind the dance itself.

The other night, for example, I went to the Club St. Hilaire, one of the best Twist temples in Paris. The floor was covered with wrenching, perspiring bodies and three of our party were trampled to death just trying to get to our table. The survivors were placed a few inches from the floor. If you are seated near the dance floor at eye level when they're doing the Twist there is always a good chance of losing an eye.

The first thing I noticed about the Club St. Hilaire dance floor was that there were more women than men on it. Apparently the girls like to do the Twist more than men do. Or maybe they're not as tired at the end of the day. The second thing I noticed was that no one was quite sure who was dancing with whom. In the Twist you are not supposed to touch your partner, and in many cases the French girls feel this gives them a license to dance with whomever they damn please.

I noted one lovely blonde who was doing the "Mess Around" with a young man, when a brunette pushed her aside and started dancing with her partner.

The blonde didn't like this, so she started dancing with someone else's partner "like she did last summer," and the party of the third part came over to our table and dragged one of our men on the floor and insisted he dance with her.

Nobody was mad at anybody except possibly the wife of the man at our table, but it would have been bad form to show it.

In the meantime I ordered drinks, but each waiter who tried to bring them was caught in the stampede, and when his body was recovered he was carried to the cash register to await a communal waiters' funeral in the morning.

It was probably my own fault because I was staring too hard, but someone swung a hip to my jaw, knocking me off my stool. I rolled on the floor, holding my head so nobody would step on it, when I discovered a lovely young thing rolling in time with me on the floor.

"That's it," she said. "You've invented a new step."

I tried to get up and she got up at the same time, but when I was knocked down again she went down, too, not missing a beat.

Another girl, realizing that we were doing something differ-

ent, pushed the other girl away and she started rolling a few feet away from me.

This time I stayed down for a count of nine and then tried to get to a neutral corner, but someone's knee caught me in the back and I was down again.

When I finally got up, all the girls wanted to twist with me, only I didn't know how to do it standing up.

One of the men in our party, who had become my manager on the spot, shouted: "Get back down on the floor."

But it was too late. The girls all left me and I crawled back to the table in disgrace.

"For a minute there," my wife said, "I thought I was married to a new Chubby Checker."

I stuck out my chin, hoping someone would knock me off the stool again, but everyone avoided the table.

"If you had only stayed on the floor," my manager said in disgust, "I could have gotten you $1,000 a week at the Peppermint Lounge."

Seventeen Years in France

DAVID SCHOENBRUN, the Columbia Broadcasting System's correspondent who has been stationed in Paris for the last seventeen years and has become one of the leading American experts on French affairs, is leaving Paris to take over as chief of bureau of the CBS Washington office. It will be a very difficult transformation for Mr. Schoenbrun, because one gets in the habit, after a while, of thinking in certain political terms, and after seventeen years it's hard to shake them.

Mr. Schoenbrun came in to see me before leaving and asked me if I would look over his first television broadcast script from Washington, D.C.

He wanted to know if I had any suggestions.

"Well, Dave," I told him quite honestly, "as you know, I'm not up on television, but are you sure you want to refer to the

Democratic Party as the Radical Left-Wing Government Majority?"

Mr. Schoenbrun said he wasn't sure.

"And you shouldn't really call the Republican Party the Fanatical Right-Wing Opposition clique."

"What do you call them?"

"The Democratic and Republican parties."

"That's all?"

"Now down here, Dave, are you certain you want to refer to the Daughters of the American Revolution as a terrorist organization?"

"You think that's too strong?"

"There could be repercussions. Let me see now. The fact that President Kennedy can't get through his old-age medical bill should not necessarily be called the worst government crisis since the question of the abolition of slavery. I think you're going out on a limb by predicting the overthrow of the Kennedy government if he doesn't get a vote of confidence on this. You see, David, in America the President stays in for four years, whether the National Assembly is hostile or not."

"That long?" Mr. Schoenbrun whistled in amazement.

"Also, David, where you're discussing some dissatisfaction among certain officers with the plan to modernize the Army, I don't think you can call them mutinous Army elements or predict that because of their disagreement there will be a putsch in the armed services in the near future."

"Well, it stands to reason," Mr. Schoenbrun said, "that if the U.S. Army isn't happy it will do *something*."

"No, David, in America when an officer is unhappy he resigns and joins the John Birch Society and goes around the country denouncing the United Nations."

"Why doesn't Kennedy throw the dissident officers in jail under Article Sixteen?"

"There is no Article Sixteen, Dave."

"No Article Sixteen? Well, how can the President deal with the rebels and the clandestine revolutionaries who are trying to topple him?"

"It's all done through Congress, David."

"What's Congress?"

"That's the lawmaking body of the American Government. You see, you've been living in France a long time, but in the United States Congress still has a lot of power."

"Well *that's* silly."

"It certainly complicates things," I admitted. "And it doesn't make your job any easier covering both Kennedy *and* Congress, but I think you're going a little strong when you refer to Kennedy as the savior of America and when you say that if he doesn't get his tariff policy through, blood will run through the streets of Washington."

"Oh, that's just an expression," Schoenbrun said. "We use it all the time about Paris. The television audiences like it."

"I'm not sure they'll like it about Washington. Otherwise, David, the script is fine. I might warn you though, that OAS in America stands for the Organization of American States and FLN stands for the Filadelphia, Lackawanna and Nashville Railroad."

A Van Dongen Poster

I HAVE this friend Alain Bernheim, and, like many friends of mine, he's much nicer to my wife than he is to me. I don't know what he thinks he is accomplishing by being nice to my wife, and I think he's beginning to wonder himself.

For example, not long ago my wife said casually that she had seen a Van Dongen poster advertising an art exhibition. She had fallen in love with it, so she said, and would give anything to have one like it.

Now Bernheim, who can find five excuses why he can't give me a light for my cigar when I ask him, pops up and says: "I'll get you the poster, my dear. Do not think about it again."

My wife smiles demurely and says: "Oh, that would be too

much trouble," which is Bernheim's cue to say: "Nothing's too much trouble for a beautiful woman."

You can imagine where I rate in my house when guys go around talking like that.

Incidentally, Bernheim's married, and his wife feels the same way about him as I do. As a matter of fact, she was the one who told me the full story of the Van Dongen poster.

It seems Bernheim had seen the poster in the window of a real estate office just across the street from the building where he works, and so during a break he dashed over and went in to ask the real estate man if he could have the poster when the exhibition was over.

The real estate man said angrily that he did not sell posters, he sold houses and apartments. Was Bernheim looking for an apartment or a house?

Bernheim, figuring he could eventually get the poster if he became friendly with the real estate man, said that's exactly what he was looking for and he just brought up the poster because he was too embarrassed to mention his search for new quarters.

"Do you want to buy the place or just the lease?"

Bernheim said he was willing to discuss the merits of each.

The real estate man brought out a series of cards.

"Here is an apartment by the Place de la République. Four rooms, central heating, one million old francs for the key, etc., etc."

They proceeded to go through the list. One hour, two hours, three hours later the man had made five appointments with Bernheim to look at places, one as far out as Rambouillet. But the poster was still securely pasted against the window.

Bernheim looked at apartments all the next week. Occasionally he brought up the subject of Van Dongen, but the real estate agent always changed it to something else. Bernheim's business suffered and his clients became peeved when they didn't find him in. But he knew it would only be a matter of time before he broke the real estate agent down.

After a week Bernheim finally couldn't take it any longer.

He had looked at 25 places, walked up 138 flights of stairs, driven 234 kilometers, and bought the real estate agent lunch every day.

"Look," said Bernheim, "about that Van Dongen poster in your window. Could I have it?"

"What a shame," the real estate agent said. "A lady came in yesterday and asked if she could have it. I wish I had known you wanted it, as I've gotten to like you very much."

There wasn't anything Bernheim could say. In France people are not embarrassed when they see a man sobbing in the street.

Anyway, his attempt to get the Van Dongen poster was not in vain. He's moving to a new apartment on Thursday.

A Little on the Table

I was invited to attend the opening of Harry Winston's new jewelry establishment in Paris on the Avenue Montaigne. The best time of the year to open a jewelry shop is September, because after all the summer jewel robberies in the south of France, most women are just getting their checks from their insurance companies and want to replenish their vaults.

The Harry Winston opening was a real society affair, to which the Duchess of Windsor and Elsa Maxwell invited us on gold-embossed invitations. Mr. Winston was donating $10,000 to the American Hospital in Paris and that's why the Duchess and Miss Maxwell agreed to get involved in what ordinarily would have been a commercial enterprise.

Miss Maxwell was obviously very sensitive about this, because the first thing she said to me when I greeted her was: "The Duchess and I are not getting anything out of this."

"Well, who said you were?" I said.

"Some people think so," Miss Maxwell harrumped. "As a matter of fact I don't like jewels. I think they're a pain in the neck. I wouldn't own jewels, not that I could afford any. I had to borrow these earrings from Harry just for the evening."

The Duchess arrived while we were talking. She was wearing a pearl necklace with diamond hearts. I asked her where the Duke was.

"He won't get a bird today," she said.

"Pardon me?"

"He's hunting. But it's too hot. No bird is going to go up in this weather."

"I don't blame him."

"Who, the Duke?"

"No, the bird."

Miss Maxwell said: "I just came back from Lebanon and I told Harry that's the place for him to open up a store. Those sheiks are the only ones who can afford this stuff."

The stuff Miss Maxwell was referring to was about $15 million worth of jewels that Mr. Winston had brought over from the United States for display at the opening.

The 250 guests started to arrive. They included Mrs. Joseph Kennedy, Mme. Henri Bonnet, Mme. Artur Rubinstein, the Maharanee of Baroda, Mrs. Gilbert Miller, Mrs. Samuel Newhouse, and Ambassador and Mrs. James Gavin.

I noticed that very few husbands showed up and I tried to find out why. A lady explained that her husband refused to come because he was afraid he was going to be touched for some money for charity.

One man had another theory. He told me: "Harry made a mistake inviting just wives. If he had invited mistresses all the husbands would have been here."

I told him to hold his tongue.

Mrs. Rolf Gerard, the wife of the set designer, was looking at some sapphires with unconcealed admiration. "Aren't they beautiful?" she asked me.

"Yes, but that diamond pin you're wearing isn't bad either."

Mrs. Gerard shrugged and sighed. "I do the best I can."

Wandering around, I discovered that a majority of the women there had been robbed at one time or another, including the Duchess of Windsor. She told me: "It was after the war when we were in England for a visit. I didn't get one thing back and I wasn't very well insured either."

Mrs. Gilbert Miller said she was robbed five years ago in England. "Since then I've been insured to the hilt. If anyone broke into my bedroom now I'd tell them to help themselves. I'm not going to risk having my teeth knocked in."

Mrs. Eve Lehman, of the Lehman banking family, said she believes in insurance. "If you're not insured the police couldn't care less. But if you're insured, the insurance companies get after them to try and get your stuff back."

I asked Ambassador Gavin if his wife had ever been robbed. The ambassador, who has been living on Army pay all his life, looked at the beautiful, but bijoux-less Mrs. Gavin and said, sadly: "It's hardly likely."

The Maharanee of Baroda, who probably has the greatest private collection of jewels in the world, said she had some good advice for people who owned jewels. "My insurance people told me to always leave a little something on the night table, like $100,000 worth, so the thieves won't get mad and hit you on the head."

Parc Monceau Intrigue

As I HAVE reported many times, the Parc Monceau, where my children are forced to play, is one of the fanciest playpens in the Western world. Only the children of the best families of France are seen in the park, and the rules are so strict that jumping, running, roller skating, and kicking sand could mean immediate arrest and military court-martial.

In such a park you're bound to find far more governesses than mothers taking care of the children. In truth, very few mothers can be found in the park, and for this reason a friend of mine has gotten herself into a situation she can't get out of.

This is what happened.

The lady, a young mother of a year-and-a-half-old boy, went

to the Parc Monceau and found herself sitting near the sand pile in the midst of a group of governesses. Since so few mothers show up at the Parc Monceau in person, the other nurses assumed my friend was also a governess and treated her as such.

My friend, too embarrassed to admit she couldn't afford a nurse for her child, pretended she was the child's nurse, and pretty soon everyone became quite friendly.

After inquiring how much money she made, the other governesses asked her how her employers treated her.

My friend revealed that she was paid a very low salary, and her employers were tyrants.

"Does she have any lovers?" one of the nannies asked.

"All the time," my friend said. "That's why she sends me to the park with the child."

"It's the same with me," one of the other nannies said.

"Does the husband give you any trouble?" another one wanted to know.

"All the time," my friend said. "He's constantly trying to get into my bedroom."

"He would, the swine," a nurse said. "The trouble is you're too young and pretty."

"Why don't you leave?" another one inquired.

"What's the difference?" my friend said. "They're all alike."

The nurses all agreed it was so.

"Who does the cooking?" one of them asked.

"I do," the friend replied.

"Don't they have a cook?" a governess asked in shocked tones.

"Yes, but she refuses to cook for me or the child."

"Our cook is the same way," a nurse said. "They think they own the house."

Every day my friend went to the park and joined the governesses. It was much more fun than sitting alone, and she even enjoyed inventing stories about her "employers."

She told them of "Madame's" latest affairs, which enthralled the other governesses, and she revealed that Monsieur was

still attempting to break down the door to her quarters without success, and each day she had a new atrocity story concerning the "cook." In no time my friend was the most popular
member of the group.

The trouble started when a few of the other governesses
offered to get my friend a date on her day off.

My friend declined, but the pressure to introduce her to
their friends was great. To complicate matters, a policeman
in the park started to pay attention to my friend and was encouraged by the other nurses in starting a romance.

There was also a retired, presumably wealthy man who had
come to know the governesses, and some of them thought he
might make a much better catch for my friend than an under-
paid policeman.

As you can see, my friend is in a terrible mess and I was
the only one she could talk to. Her husband would never
understand, and on Sunday she's had to find excuses not to
take the child to the park. Also her son is starting to talk
and she lives in fear he will one day call her Mamma.

The only thing I could advise my friend to do was move
to another neighborhood. But it's a lesson to all of us. You
start fooling around in the Parc Monceau and they're bound
to catch up with you sooner or later.

That's one of the reasons it's one of the best-run parks in
the world.

7.
Is It Safe To Visit
the U.S.A.?

Anyone for Lecturing?

I was invited to go out on a lecture tour of the United States under the auspices of the Columbia Lecture Bureau, a professional booking agency which sends speakers out to banquet halls, auditoriums, universities, executive clubs, and whoever else will pay the ridiculously low fee to hear me.

This is the first time I've done this sort of thing as a professional and I must say it is an interesting experience. Lecturing, according to insurance statistics, is among the most hazardous professions in the United States, and only seven of every ten speakers ever return from a tour. The rest expire somewhere along the way, usually of chicken à la king poisoning, cocktail-party tremors, or wounds inflicted during the question period which inevitably follows the talks.

As a member of this dangerous speakers' foreign legion I'd like to tell you a little about what happens to those of us who speak for our supper.

First of all, most organizations have committees to decide what speakers they will invite to grace the podium. All lecture bureaus send out catalogues at the beginning of the year similar to the "wanted" posters put out by the FBI, with a picture of the speaker, what he will talk about, and a few quotes from the president of the Kiwanis Club of Fort Wayne, Indiana, where he spoke four years ago so successfully.

If enough committees want you, then you are booked on what is known as a "lecture tour."

The lecture bureau arranges your transportation, your hotel accommodations, and issues you your backbreaking schedule. They always pay you after the series is over just in case you're one of the three out of ten who never gets back.

Now giving a lecture is probably the easiest work a person can do. You stand up in front of a microphone and talk for an hour, no more, with authority, and everyone is very impressed that they're getting so much from the horse's mouth. It pays to be dull for a certain part of the talk, because if you're booked as a humorous speaker, and you're not dull, people will think you aren't serious.

It is before-the-speech and after-the-speech that life is so tough for a lecturer.

A lecturer who comes to a small town is very much sought after socially, and people just can't entertain you enough. As a matter of fact you usually discover the program chairman and president of the organization you're addressing aren't speaking to each other, because they both wanted to give you a cocktail party on the same night.

Lecturers, for some reason, always seem to attract the town alcoholics and it isn't long before you find yourself being pushed in a corner by either a man or a woman who is telling you he never read your stuff and he doesn't like it anyway, and if you really want a good article you ought to write about the new shopping center going up on High Street.

If you can escape from him you wind up playing a game called "Do you know?" No matter what part of America I've visited I always run into somebody who knows somebody who lived in Paris ten years ago. You can imagine what a bum I am if I don't know their friend, who claims to have been my best friend while he lived in the French capital.

The best audiences from a lecturer's point of view are students, the worst are women's groups. Women are afraid to laugh out loud when they're sitting with other women, and under each heart of gold at a women's luncheon lies a face of stone.

U. S. Is Short of Reds

AFTER lecturing in many parts of the United States the one thing that has struck me is how vigilant every community has become toward the problem of Communism. There has not been a town I've hit on my tour that doesn't have at least four organizations working night and day to repel the Communist threat in the United States, which, as all vigilantes know, is getting more serious as each United Nations session goes by.

Unhappily, while there are more organizations being formed to fight Communists in the United States, there are less and less Communists around to fight, and the anti-Communist organizations are fighting among themselves over who has a right to fight the Communists.

Many of the smaller towns, particularly in the South, have the strongest anti-Communist organizations, despite the fact that they are so far off the beaten track that many of them have never seen a Communist. In Waco, Texas, for example, the nearest card-holding Communist Party member lives in Dallas, a hundred miles away. While Waco stands at the ready to repulse the infidel, the Communist Party member has been warned not to leave Dallas, as the anti-Communist organizations there claim that since he lives in Dallas he belongs to them.

Sarasota, Florida, seems to have the same problem. The threat of the Communists taking over Sarasota hangs heavy over the heads of some of the leaders of this beautiful city, and the printing presses are grinding out tons of paper warning of the impending invasion. In the meantime, members of the Communist Party keep passing up Sarasota, preferring to spend their winters in Palm Beach. Sarasota, despite its ideal location for internal subversion, has been unable to attract any Communists for the anti-Communists to attack.

Other towns throughout the United States have also suffered from the unwillingness of the Communists to show up, and the problem is playing havoc with the defense of the American way of life.

It is true that most of the ultraconservative anti-Communists are not as concerned with attacking Communists as they are with attacking people who are not Communists but think like Communists, or, to put it another way, think differently than the anti-Communists do.

But this leads to complications, because when you get past the names of former President Eisenhower, Chief Justice Earl Warren, Mrs. Roosevelt, and Adlai Stevenson, no one can agree on who else represents a Communist threat in the United States.

Therefore, rather than drive the Communist Party underground in America, which isn't helping anyone, I think the Communist Party members should be redistributed around the country so that every town can have at least one. Having a Communist of their very own would make the anti-Communists less frustrated, and they wouldn't be fighting among themselves over who is and who is not a Communist.

The Communist who is willing to move to one of these towns would be well paid by the anti-Communist organizations, who have so much money to spend they would pay anything to get a Communist to live in their town.

Everyone would be happy. The Communist would receive a good salary for living in the town, and the town would have a reason for having so many anti-Communist organizations.

It's the only solution to the terrible Communist shortage in the United States. While the big cities might object to losing their Communists, I think the smaller communities have a right to have some Communists, too.

François Writes Pierre

My cher Pierre,

Please forgive me for not writing sooner but I have been in my fallout shelter for the last four months and haven't been able to post any letters. You see, what happened was that when President Kennedy told us we all better go into our fallout shelters because of Berlin, we went. But the trouble was nobody told us when to come out. I kept waiting for an all-clear signal or maybe a visit from an air-raid warden, but absolutely no one came, so Yvonne and the children and I decided to stick it out. But after four months we drank up all the Pernod and I decided I better come up and have a look around.

You can imagine my surprise when I discovered New York was not even damaged, and there was plenty of water and food for everybody. Then I started to make some discreet inquiries. I discovered that although the Berlin crisis was by no means over, the government thought it was better if everybody went back to work instead of guarding their shelters. But nobody thought to tell me. I suppose it's because I'm a Frenchman and the Americans have to think of their own first.

The experience in the fallout shelter wasn't too bad. Yvonne fixed it up very nice with Louis XV furniture; I designed the wine cellar, and we stocked up on cassoulet, bouillabaisse, crêpes, and fromage. It cost a pretty franc, I can tell you. As a matter of fact, if I had to do it all over, I would have listened to my friend.

He told me: "Look, François. Your shelter cost you $4,800. It cost another $2,000 to furnish it, and $3,000 for air conditioning, plumbing, electricity, and television. Why don't you just spend $55 for a shotgun and then if anything happens you can impose on your neighbors to go into theirs. It will save you so much money and bother."

But Yvonne wouldn't hear of it. She's seen our neighbor's fallout shelter and she thinks it's been furnished atrociously. She can't understand what people see in modern.

The children were wonderful during the four months. We went down with five and we have two left.

François, Jr., throttled little Jacques on the third day over who had a right to sleep in the upper bunk. I became very angry with François, Jr., about this, but François has been around American kids too long and all he would say was: "You never take my side and you are not interested in my problems." I pointed out throttling his brother over an upper

bunk in a fallout shelter wasn't exactly a nice thing to do and
he replied: "Teen-agers have some rights, too."

After two weeks, little Philippe and Charles became bored
and started to play a game of who could hold his breath the
longest. They became so intent on winning that they both
expired before I could stop them.

So now there is only François, Jr., little Jeanette, Yvonne,
and myself. We never believed in large families anyway.

François, Jr., became very mad at me when he came out
of the shelter and realized we had wasted so much time.
According to him, he missed three gang rumbles and one
dance at the YMCA.

I have read in the papers you are having a lot of trouble
in France now, and I am sorry to hear this, but whatever you
do don't build a fallout shelter. It isn't the closeness of quarters or even being underground for such a long time that will
get you. It's drinking the wine at room temperature.

Your cher ami,
François

Secretaries Run U.S.

EVERY time I come back to the United States for a short visit
something strikes me about the American scene that I hadn't
noticed before.

This time the thing that hit me was how powerful the
American secretary has become in the American way of life.

I hadn't realized it until I tried to make an appointment
with a successful college chum who was pulling down around
$40,000 a year in a big company (which shall remain name-
less, as his secretary would never forgive him for speaking to
me about her).

After several attempts I finally managed to get a luncheon
date and he apologized profusely for the difficulty I had
experienced.

"You don't understand what's going on in the United

States," he told me, looking around to make sure no one was listening. "The secretaries are taking over. No one can get through to me if my secretary decides she doesn't want him to.

"She makes all my apopintments, she decides when I can take a vacation, if it's safe for me to make a speech in another town. She watches me constantly, and I swear I'm scared silly of her."

"Why don't you fire her?" I asked him.

He looked at me incredulously. "You must be out of your mind. You can't fire your secretary. She knows where all the bodies are buried. She's my espionage agent to let me know what's going on in the company.

"Without the information she picks up from the other secretaries I wouldn't be able to last a week with the company. Besides, frankly, I don't understand what I'm supposed to be doing in the company, and she does."

"I can see your point," I said, watching him drink his third martini.

He stared into the glass. "The only thing is, I wish she wouldn't hate my wife so."

"Does she hate your wife?"

"All secretaries hate their bosses' wives," he said. "I don't think it has anything to do with jealousy. It's just that secretaries think wives are so damn inefficient. They feel that wives also take up too much of their bosses' time. My secretary thinks that I could do a much better job if I didn't have to go home to my wife for dinner. And she believes my weekends with my family are a complete waste of time. She doesn't see how I can live with a woman who doesn't understand the company.

"Also, since my secretary pays all the bills, she thinks my wife is sort of a spendthrift. But to be honest, I'm so browbeaten by my secretary during the day, with her constant nagging and efficiency, that I really look forward to going home to my wife at night. I look on my wife as a sort of a mistress, the only one who understands me."

"What does your wife think about your secretary?"

"She's afraid of my secretary. My wife has to be nice to her, because if she isn't, my secretary won't let my wife speak to me. As it is, my secretary only lets her get through 50 per cent of the time. The other 50 per cent she just says I'm in an important meeting, as if to imply my wife should know better than to call the office when world-shaking events are going on behind the company's locked doors."

"I didn't realize secretaries were that powerful," I said sympathetically.

"You don't know the half of it. Look, if your secretary catches a cold and is out two days, you might as well shoot yourself. But if your wife catches penumonia, all you have to do is come to the office and tell your secretary to notify Blue Cross."

Victory by Telephone

MR. THEODORE FLICKER, the impresario of the very success-ful off-Broadway satirical theater "The Premise," is one of the few people I know who has never lost an argument to the telephone company. Mr. Flicker carries a grudge against the phone company because, being in the theater, he feels that the phone company discriminates against actors and actresses.

"An actor or an actress," Mr. Flicker said, "being self-employed has to pay a much higher deposit on a phone than anybody else and I think it's unfair, because without a phone an actress or actor can't get work."

Mr. Flicker's greatest victory against the phone company came a few years back when he was rooming with a writer in New York named Peter Stone.

They had rented a telephone-answering machine from the phone company for $12.50 a month. It was a tape machine and you could leave messages on it when someone called you and you were out.

Mr. Flicker would leave the voice of an irritable Japanese houseboy on the machine and when someone called the voice would say: "Sh-sh-sh. You clazy or something callin' boss at this hour? He asleep sleep, no take calls for five hours, good-by." Click.

Or Mr. Stone would record Jimmy Stewart's voice from an old movie on television just at the moment when Mr. Stewart would say: "Hi, thar, glad you could come to town." Click. Or Lauren Bacall: "I don't care how many times you said you love me. Say it again. This is a recorded announcement." Click.

Well, you can imagine the fun Mr. Flicker and Mr. Stone had with their machine. But finally the day came when they decided to give it up and return it to the telephone company. They called the phone company and asked them to disconnect the machine and take it away. The phone company sent someone over to disconnect it. But the person who was supposed to take it away never showed up.

Days passed, then weeks, then months and the machine stood there on a table. Calls to the phone company produced no results so finally Mr. Flicker called and said: "I know you're having difficulty getting over here to pick up your machine so I'm going to make it easy for you. If you're not here by five o'clock I'm going to leave your machine on the sidewalk in front of my apartment and you can pick it up there."

The tape-recording machine was picked up in an hour.

But as far as Messieurs Flicker and Stone are concerned this was not the end of the affair. Mr. Stone and Mr. Flicker wrote a letter to the phone company and said:

> We had your telephone-answering machine for six months and while it was in use it was well worth the $12.50 a month. But when it was disconnected it was not rendering us a service; in fact we were rendering the telephone company a service by storing for them one nonworking telephone-answering machine.
>
> Our price for this storage is $12.50 a month and therefore

you owe us $37.50. While we are not ordinarily in the tele-phone-answering-machine storage business, we will be very happy to store as many machines at the rate of $12.50 each per month as can be stored in our apartment. Please advise as to how many you wish to store as it will take time for the contractors to complete the necessary shelving and for us to find a new apartment in which to live. Sincerely yours.

The next day they received a call from a man at the phone company who chortled on the phone and said that although they couldn't deduct the rent from the bill, they could hand in a separate bill, which he pointed out the telephone company would probably refuse to pay and would instead fight in court with the many lawyers they kept on retainer for just such emergencies.

Mr. Flicker then replied that he expected as much from a company which was a "monopoly." The magic word monop-oly was all he needed before the phone company offered to settle out of court for the largest item on the Flicker-Stone phone bill of the previous month—a call to Paris which cost $24.

On the basis of their experience, Mr. Flicker has a theory that the phone company is really a supranational power above everything.

"First there was chaos and then there was the phone com-pany," he told me. "The phone company owns everything and that's why I'm sure there won't be a war. The company wouldn't permit it because it would damage too much of their equipment."

Charity Starts in Florida

OF ALL the communities in the United States there is prob-ably none as social as Palm Beach, Florida. This sun-drenched, diamond-studded, Rolls-Royce-clogged stretch of real estate has more cocktail and dinner parties per capita than any other town in the free world.

There is a society editor for every five families in the colony, as opposed to the national average of one for every hundred families. But Palm Beach is not social just for the sake of being social. All the society activity down here has to do with raising money for some charity. It is very gauche to have a party for the sake of a party, and therefore everyone is in the business of giving a party for a cause.

It's gotten so that two people can't have breakfast together without making a donation to an orphanage.

As a matter of fact, while there is no shortage of parties and balls in Palm Beach, there is a shortage of diseases to give them for. The oldtimers in Palm Beach have all the good diseases tied up. The first families of this city have a monopoly on heart, cancer, cerebral palsy, and mental health, and a newcomer who is trying to crash society down here has very few illnesses left to choose from.

The other day I asked four friends to have lunch with me, and one of them, Mrs. Paul Ames, asked: "What's it for?"

"Nothing," I said. "We just want to have lunch."

"You can't just have lunch without a reason," she said. "If you can come up with a good disease, we'll accept."

I called the local Palm Beach hospital and asked them if there were any diseases that there hadn't been benefits held for this season.

"You're calling awfully late," the woman said. "The only thing we still have open is malaria and yellow fever."

"Is arthritis taken?" I asked.

"It was one of the first to go. We can't give you diabetes or hay fever, either."

"Well, is there some hospital I could raise money for?"

"We have an animal shelter in Cheyenne, Wyoming, that hasn't been spoken for."

"Okay, I'll give a luncheon for that. What do I do now?"

"You have to form a committee."

"What for?"

"To get your wife's picture in the newspaper. Why else would you want to give a benefit?"

"That's true," I said.

"Just call the local newspaper and they'll send a photographer over in ten minutes."

I formed a committee consisting of my wife as honorary chairman, Mrs. Ames as program chairman, and Mrs. Howard Gould, of Cincinnati, as decorations chairman.

After the newspaper photographers took their pictures, I took the women and their husbands in to lunch in the coffee shop of the Palm Beach Towers, where we all were staying.

Unfortunately the coffee shop was very crowded and we had to share our table with three other couples whom we didn't know.

But it worked out fine because the three couples each pledged $1,000 for our animal shelter in Cheyenne and our party in turn bought $3,000 in raffle tickets that they were selling for a retired lifeguards' home in Seattle, Washington.

Somewhere in Florida

THE magic word in Florida these days is "land." According to the exciting advertisements on the highways, in newspapers and magazines, anyone who is willing to plunk $10 down and pay $10 a month can in no time at all become another William Zeckendorf or Conrad Hilton.

No matter who you are, the land fever grips you as soon as you get off the plane, and I must admit I was no exception. Not wanting to be left out of what is potentially the greatest "growth investment in the United States" since fallout shelters, I swiped ten bucks from my kid's toy bank and rushed out to the neaerst real-estate development office (there are about two on every block).

The office, located in a vacated store, was very plush. There were photos of beautiful homes on the wall—which, I discovered later, had nothing to do with the development, but gave the place a nice atmosphere.

A gorgeous receptionist was typing up mortgages, but when she saw the ten dollars I was clutching in my hand, she immediately ushered me into the plush office of the managing director. The director, a jovial man in a Palm Beach suit, shook my hand vigorously and invited me to sit in one of his plush chairs. On his desk was a mock-up, in scale, of his latest development, an entire town. The mock-up showed three golf courses, five schools, a church, a yacht club and basin, and five hundred ranch-type houses.

I gasped when I looked at it.

"You're very lucky," he said. "We have only one house left."

"Could I go out and see it?" I asked excitedly.

"Why would you want to do that?" he asked. "Don't you believe what you see here on my desk?"

"Well, it is beautiful," I said. "But I thought it would be fun to go out and see the place for myself, size up my neighbors and that sort of thing."

"It's a pretty long trip," he said. "You see, we built this town in the Everglades to get away from all those jet noises people are always complaining about. It's about a hundred miles inland, but you can only travel by day because of the alligators."

"Alligators?"

"Of course. You have to have alligators to eat the moccasin snakes, or they'd be all over the place."

"Snakes?"

"Only during the wet season," he said. "You hardly ever see them unless there's a wildcat around."

"Wildcats?"

"They won't give you any trouble unless you get caught in the quicksand."

"Quicksand?"

"Only in certain places. We have a couple of patches by

the school, but the teacher usually keeps the kids away from them. Now if you'll just sign this paper."

"Wait a minute," I said. "I'm not sure I want to live in the Everglades, and, besides, are you sure the town exists as you have it there?"

"It's not completed yet, but we've already sprayed the malaria mosquito ponds, and by next month we should have the wild-boar traps all dug. In a year it will look just like this mock-up."

"You mean the church isn't even built yet?"

"Well, no. But don't forget this is the church of your choice, and if it was already built, it wouldn't be the church of your choice then, would it?"

I admitted that was true. Just then the phone rang and he picked it up. I couldn't help overhearing the conversation.

"Yes sir, Mr. Ford. You'd like to build a factory on my tract? It's going to be difficult. I have a man in my office now and I've already promised him the last five acres. No, I can't give you his name. But perhaps he'll get in touch with you. Sorry. Good-by."

I plunked down the ten dollars and hurriedly signed the deed.

I've been trying to get in touch with Mr. Ford ever since, but he always seems to be out. Once I get him on the phone, though, and tell him about the land I own, he's really going to have to pay through the nose.

Puff, Puff, Puff, Puff

THE problem of getting good Cuban cigars is starting to become serious. President Kennedy put an embargo on them without consulting any cigar smokers, because he knew what the response of a cigar smoker would be in regard to Castro:

"Anyone who makes a good Havana cigar can't be all bad."

But a cigar smoker is a desperate man when he can't get

the cigar he wants and will go to any measures to satisfy his taste buds. Plans are already under way to get cigars by hook or by crook.

I went into a cigar store the other evening and asked for a Havana. The man said he didn't have any, but if I would wait on the street corner a few minutes he might arrange for me to get a box.

In about ten minutes a black Cadillac pulled up and the driver whistled a few bars of "Smoke Gets in Your Eyes." I hopped into the car, and while one person blindfolded me the other drove in what seemed to be the direction of Long Island.

When we got about seventy-five miles out we stopped at a little cove and the blindfold was taken off. One of the men pulled a small searchlight out and started flashing signals.

In a moment a fast speedboat roared into the dock, picked me up, and raced back into the darkness.

The speedboat took me exactly twelve miles out and stopped at a big green freighter.

Several men trained their machine guns on me and I was led to a cabin.

There I came face to face with the notorious cigar bootlegger, "Dutch" Master.

Dutch was in an expansive mood. He told me he hadn't worked since 1933, when Prohibition was repealed. "This Kennedy act is a noble experiment," he said. "Bootlegging had become a depressed industry, but now we have full employment."

"How do you plan to smuggle your cigars into the United States?" I asked.

He ripped open a case which was lettered SCOTCH WHISKY. Inside was nothing but Cuban cigars. "The Federals will never get wise," he said.

"Won't the Kennedy Administration let any cigars into the country legally?" I asked him.

"Yes," he said. "But only for 'medicinal' purposes and you've got to have a doctor's prescription."

I bought a couple of boxes and then told Dutch I thought it was a long trip to make every time.

"Don't worry," he said. "We're starting a series of speak-easies for cigar smokers. Here, take this card. The password is 'Churchill sent me.'"

I was blindfolded again and then driven back into town. A few days later I decided to visit the address Dutch had given me. It was a brownstone house and all the window shades were drawn.

I rang the bell and said the password. The door opened and I was hustled inside.

When my eyes got adjusted to the light I discovered I was in a large room filled with big club chairs and men drawing on long Havana cigars while they read their *Fortune* magazines.

"What are all these men doing here?" I asked an attendant who was carrying a murderous cigar clipper.

His eyes were glazed and happy. "Making whoopee," he said.

Sculpture in Food

I MET a man who has one of the most interesting and at the same time frustrating jobs in New York City. Mr. Jon W. Schwartz is a free-lance food sculptor. He works for caterers in New York as well as himself and receives commissions to design and sculpture food works of art for all occasions.

One of Mr. Schwartz's favorite mediums is chicken liver. He has made houses of chicken liver for housewarming parties, a desk and chair of chicken liver for a man who received a promotion in his company, a champagne slipper of chicken liver for a sweet-sixteen party, and a kangaroo of chicken liver for someone who was coming home from Australia.

"I use the best chicken liver I can get," he told me, "and I add onions and eggs, which gives the form substance. My statues are not just decorative—they're to be eaten."

Mr. Schwartz got into the free-lance business because he felt standard molds at catered parties were getting old-fashioned and people wanted something more inspired—some food decoration that they could call their own.

Mr. Schwartz is called in on every type of party. Recently he was asked to think up something nice for a party a couple were giving for their dog, which had just graduated from a training school. Mr. Schwartz designed the school in chopped chicken liver and the dog was made of Ken-L Ration. Later on, the real dog was given the statue to eat.

Another time, Mr. Schwartz was asked by a lady decorator to do a model apartment, made to scale, of food. He used beef Stroganoff for the bed, turnips for the bathroom utilities. The chairs in the living room were carved out of squash and filled with chicken à la king, and his rugs were made of crackers. It took him three days to do the model, and he was paid $1,000 for it.

"Everything is on a personal level," Mr. Schwartz told me. "I have to think what the party is for, what the people are like, if it's a sad occasion or a happy occasion or . . ."

"What do you mean, a sad occasion?" I asked him.

"Well, not long ago I was asked to design something for a party for a son who was going away into the Army. It was a sad occasion, so I took him, through the medium of food, leaving his house, made of chopped chicken liver, traveling on a train carved from pineapple fried in deep fat, to the moment he meets his first sergeant, who is a turkey. The boy himself was a potato, which I used in several scenes. The parents wept when they saw it."

Once Mr. Schwartz catered to a party of two. "A young lady wanted to get her boy friend, who was coming home on leave from the Army, to propose to her, but she didn't have the nerve to ask him, so she decided to do it with food. I designed a table with a church made of celery and mashed potatoes at one end, and at the other end a house made of tuna fish with three little children, also made of tuna fish, playing outside. In between were rose petals and candles. Her boy friend got the message and he asked the girl to marry him. It only cost her $150."

But sometimes Mr. Schwartz's creations don't have a happy ending. One married couple who were breaking up were talked into getting back together again by their lawyers, and they decided to have a party to celebrate. Mr. Schwartz was called in by the wife to design something special for the occasion. She chose as her theme the place in Maine where the couple honeymooned and had Mr. Schwartz make a replica of it in shrimp salad with a Maine lake made of fruit punch. The forest was made of olives and parsley. Everything was fine until the table was rolled out into the living room.

The husband took one look at it and said, "Aw the hell with it," and walked out of the house and got a divorce.

Fitness in Washington

EVER since President Kennedy announced his physical fitness program and urged Americans to get into shape, health clubs have been opening all across the nation. One of the most original ones is the new Nick Canny Gym in Washington, which combines physical fitness with political vigor and is aimed at the busy Washington politician who doesn't have too much time to spare.

I was given a tour of the health club by Mr. Canny himself. It was doing a tremendous business, and every corner of the premises, which incidentally houses one of the largest gyms in the country, had heaving, perspiring men in sweatshirts working out.

Mr. Canny took me to one side, where several men were throwing something. I couldn't make out exactly what it was.

"What are they doing?" I asked.

"They're Congressmen," Mr. Canny explained, "and they're hurling invectives."

"All of them?" I asked.

"No," Mr. Canny replied. "Those two over there are actually throwing caution to the wind. We give them their choice— whichever they find easier."

We walked on a little further and came upon a small group who seemed to be off balance.

When I looked at them questioningly, Mr. Canny explained: "These are Congressional liaison men from the various executive branches of government. They're practicing leaning over backward to please the people over there who are hurling the invectives."

I heard some grunting, and I turned around to see several men writhing on mats.

Mr. Canny said: "Those are paid lobbyists who are wrestling with their consciences."

"Who wins?"

"Not one of those men has ever lost a match."

Farther on I saw some men flying through the air.

"What are they doing?"

"They're from a Senate investigation committee," Mr. Canny said, "and they're jumping to conclusions."

"Over there we have different equipment for body building. Those parallel bars are for stretching the truth, and other bars are to practice straddling an issue. And those are stumbling blocks which they have to avoid."

I saw several men in a corner hopping up and down, and going backward and forward.

"What the devil are they doing?" I asked.

"They're newcomers to Washington," Mr. Canny said, "and they're throwing their weight around."

Next to the main gym was a smaller room which was filled with all sorts of weird equipment. One of the machines looked like a saw that woodsmen use to cut down trees. Two men in sweatshirts were working it back and forth.

"What are they up to?"

"They're two newspapermen from the National Press Club who are cutting a long story short."

"What's that man doing next to them?"

"He's a Senator from one of the silver states and he has an ax to grind."

"Oh," I said. "This is most interesting."

"It makes the men feel they aren't wasting their time," Mr. Canny said. "Would you like to see the swimming pool?"

"Very much."

It was a beautiful pool, very long and very wide, and there were many men in it.

Mr. Canny pointed to the first group, who kept diving under water: "They're practicing ducking the issue."

"And that group there?"

"These are just poor State Department career men who are trying to keep their heads above water."

The last group really perplexed me. A group of men kept putting sandbags in the water.

"What are they up to?"

"They're a team of New Frontiersmen who are damning everyone with faint praise."

White House Pickets

NOT everybody knows it, but anyone can picket the White House, the home of the President of the United States, and from the looks of things more people are doing it all the time.

In recent months, ever since the Ban the Bomb supporters have gone into action, all picketing records at the White House have been broken, possibly because the people doing the picketing feel the President cares.

Forgetting the subject matter, I did a slight bit of research on how to preceed if you want to picket the President's home. First of all, the Constitution provides you can picket without a permit, which is just as well, since a police officer in Washington told me: "If you needed a permit I assure you I would let no one picket the President's house. It's indecent."

When you decide to picket the White House you must follow certain ground rules laid down by the Washington, D.C., Police Department, which is charged with keeping pickets in line.

For one thing, they assign you the sidewalk space for your particular picket; the amount of sidewalk allotted to you is usually based on the size of the group. If the group is too large, you may be asked to picket across the street or down by the Treasury Building. Sometimes there are pickets protesting an issue and counterpickets protesting the pickets. Every time the Ban the Bomb people picket, another group shows up which pickets them and calls for Peace Through Strength.

Much to the consternation of the police, whose sympathies are against pickets of all kinds, the President recently sent out two five-gallon jugs of coffee for the anti-nuclear-testing group, which led one police captain to mutter that allowing pickets to picket the White House was bad enough, but giving them coffee was going too far.

When you picket the White House, you're not allowed to yell, shout, sing, or make any noise. You must keep moving at all times and can't sit down, stop for lunch, take a drink of any alcoholic beverage, or feed the squirrels on the White House lawn.

You can't stop anyone who is walking by, and if you give him a handbill and he throws it to the ground, you must pick it up or you will be arrested for littering the sidewalk.

Also, spitting on the sidewalk is a serious offense.

There are two kinds of picketing at the White House—group picketing and individual picketing. Group picketing is the most common, and busloads of people are now arriving every day in Washington for the specific purpose of protesting at 1600 Pennsylvania Avenue.

At the same time there are individual pickets who come out every day with their signs and stroll up and down for a few hours, complaining about anything from poisoned bread to public-affairs shows on television.

The chance of President Kennedy's seeing someone picket the White House or reading a picket sign is minimal. President Kennedy's office does not overlook Pennsylvania Avenue, and unless he looks out at lunchtime from the dining-room window it's doubtful that he'll see any pickets in action.

By the same token, the chances are good that Caroline will be watching you picket the White House, although it doesn't help much, since she can't read.

If you can't come to Washington yourself, you can always get someone to picket for you. There are now many professional pickets in Washington who, according to the police, come out for a different cause each day. I was unable to get the rates for professional pickets, but it is said to be about ten dollars a day, plus the cost of the sign.

In doing research on the story I made a phone call from my Washington hotel to the police department. It was 8:30 in the morning, and when I gave the number of the police station the operator asked me if there was anything wrong.

I said there wasn't and I would like the police.

The next voice I heard was that of the assistant manager, who wanted to know if I had been robbed. I said I hadn't and all I wanted was the police department.

He said: "Would you rather come down and talk to me?"

I said I wouldn't and, after pleading some more, he finally let the operator place the call. When I completed it I went down to the White House and picketed in protest over the fact that if you want to call the police in Washington, D.C., the hotel where you're staying won't let you.

Dow Jones Social Averages

WASHINGTON is the most social-conscious city in the world, and your status in the nation's capital depends on where you have been invited for cocktails or dinner and by whom.

In the previous administrations you received points if you were asked to the home of a senator or a Supreme Court justice or even a Cabinet member.

Since the Eisenhowers rarely entertained, the point spread was on a much lower level and the scoring was very complicated.

But all this has changed during the Kennedy Administration. Since the Kennedys came to Washington, the only important social activity anyone is interested in has to do with the White House, and a whole new set of rules has been instituted on the Dow Jones social averages.

This is how it goes.

If you're invited for a state dinner at the White House to hear Pablo Casals, you get four points.

If you're invited to a private dinner at the White House and asked to stay for the evening, you get six points. If you're asked to come in after dinner for dancing, three points, but you get an extra point if it turns into a Twist party.

If the President dances with your wife or if you dance with Mrs. Kennedy, you automatically get twenty points.

The only way you can get more points than this is if your child is invited to a birthday party for Caroline.

You get twenty-five points for this and an extra five points if your kid is also in Caroline's dancing class.

President Kennedy has been responsible for some radical changes in Washington's social playing fields. Previous to his Administration the highest honor you could receive in Washington was to be invited to the White House for dinner. But now if the President comes to your house it counts more. You get ten points if he accepts an invitation beforehand, and fifteen if he drops in unannounced.

Being invited to the Vice-President's house does not have the point value you might think it would. The Vice-President entertains so much and shows up at so many parties that it's only worth two points. As a matter of fact, most people automatically start off with two points, thanks to Lady Bird's fame as a hostess.

After President Kennedy's, the most sought-after invitations are those given by Robert and Ethel Kennedy. You get ten points if you're invited to their house, and an extra seven if you're thrown in the swimming pool with your clothes on.

Dinner with any of the other Kennedys is worth eight points unless you play touch football, in which case you're entitled to another three or the equivalent of a free kick.

In this Administration, Cabinet members' dinners are only worth one point, unless a member of the Kennedy family is present—then you get a bonus of half a point.

Ambassadors used to rate very high in Washington, but now there are so many of them here it doesn't really mean much. You can get a point if you are invited to British Ambassador Ormsby Gore's residence and possibly a point if you are asked to French Ambassador Hervé Alphand's house, but the scorers are reluctant to give anything for any of the other ambassadors, with one exception.

If you go to a Washington restaurant with an ambassador from one of the African countries and you get served, you get fifty points.

Since the year has hardly started, no one knows who will wind up with the highest score. Leading so far is a close friend of Mr. Kennedy's who was in the South Pacific with him during the war, went to Harvard, and just gave the White House a dining-room set that once belonged to Rutherford B. Hayes.

Peace Corpsmen's VA

NOBODY realizes it, but by next year many Peace Corps volunteers who have served their time abroad will be returning to the United States to be given honorable discharges. If the Peace Corps veterans are anything like other American vets they will present a problem, and I finally met a man who has been worrying about it.

Mr. Marvin Kitman, a writer, has formed a nonprofit organization of volunteers called the Peace Corps Veterans' Administration. Mr. Kitman told me his organization is prepared to help Peace Corps veterans find their way back to the American way of life.

"We're not concerned about them finding jobs," Mr. Kitman said. "After all, Peace Corpsmen will have been working for two years at salaries ranging from $60 a month in Nigeria to $182 a month in Tanganyika. There are plenty of jobs in the United States in that pay range.

"The problem the Peace Corps veteran will face is readjusting to America again. For two years he has lived like the natives, eating their foods, living in their huts, doctoring himself with native medicines, and sleeping on straw mats.

"By the time they come back to the States, nine out of ten PC vets will despise the flabby Americans they will find in their homes, their schools, and the church of their choice.

"What is even worse, they will feel we don't understand them, and since they've been speaking Swahili, Tagalog, Urdu, and Twi for two years, we probably won't.

"Clearly the average PC vet will be as restless as a Congo native, and will be in no shape to be turned loose on the American public without an intensive orientation program.

"Our organization intends to set up Displaced Peace Corpsmen camps. To wean them away from the thatch-hut architecture the veterans have grown to love, the DPC camps will be composed of split-level ranches and Cape Cod houses located on gently curving streets.

"The primary job of the DPC camps will be rehabilitation. The DPCs will have to be taught how to use knives and forks again, how to sit on chairs, how to knot a tie, and how to write something besides an inflammatory postcard to their friends back home."

Mr. Kitman said one of the most urgent problems the camps would deal with was to make the PC veteran understand the value of American money.

"Sargent Shriver has said the Peace Corpsmen will receive a bonus on return to the States, depending on the number of months he has spent overseas. In most cases it will amount to around $1,800.

"If the veterans get the money outright, some of them used to living in the bush could make this sum last eight years. They would knock the hell out of the entire American economy.

"Therefore the camp will show nothing but television commercials to get the veteran to start spending his money again at the same rate as his fellow Americans."

Mr. Kitman said his organization, like all veterans' organizations, intends to have a Peace Corps Veterans' Day at which time Peace Corps vets will hold parades in depressed areas all over the United States.

"The PCVA will also provide legal assistance for vets who have been arrested for trying to work sixteen hours a day and weekends as they did in Sierra Leone. No country that's talking about a five-hour day can allow people to work that long without putting them in jail."

I asked Mr. Kitman how he got interested in the Peace Corps Veterans Administration, and he told me: "I have a friend in the Peace Corps and he came home on a short leave and we were walking down Fifty-sixth Street one afternoon and he saw a hole dug by Consolidated Edison, so he stopped, grabbed a shovel, and started filling it in. It was such a reflex action that I said to myself: 'Some day these boys are going to need help.'"

Columbus's Countdown

I WAS very impressed with the television coverage of Lieutenant Colonel Glenn's flight into orbit, which covered every facet, not only of the trip itself, but of Colonel Glenn's private life, and it got me to thinking. I wonder how television would have covered Christopher Columbus's departure from Spain when he went off into the unknown to discover the New World.

This is what might have happened:

"Good morning everybody, this is Don Carlos Vicente Henriquez Pietro San Pedro Juarez, your anchor man on the Castilian Broadcasting System, and this is August 3, 1492, a big morning for all of us. After countless delays which have taken seven years, Christopher Columbus is ready to sail into the unknown, to find a new route to the Indies. But let's first go down to Palos de la Frontera, where hundreds of reporters from all over the world are gathered to see the departure of the *Santa María,* the *Pinta,* and the *Niña.* Let's switch to Don Alfredo, who is on the scene. Don, would you tell us a little about the craft that are going to take Chris into the unknown?"

(Shot of port of Palos de la Frontera.)

"Thanks, Don Carlos. Well, folks, as you can imagine, this is an exciting day for all of us, and, as you can see in the distance, there is the *Santa María,* the *Niña,* and the *Pinta,* which are now being fueled as the countdown approaches. I have standing next to me the foreman of the shipyard and he can probably tell us a little about the ships. Señor Fernandez, would you tell the audience about the *Santa María,* the craft that Chris will be sailing in?"

"Well, Don, it weighs one hundred tons or double hogsheads of wine. We've put in a mainmast, and an immense square sail which will do most of the driving. Then we have a small main topsail for emergencies, and, as you can see, there's a mizzenmast stepped on the high poop which carries a small lateen-rigged sail, and there is a bowspirit sail as well. We've included every safety feature that is known to modern man."

"I'm sure you have, Señor Fernandez, and I might say now that thousands of people have been working years to make this moment possible, and I think Chris Columbus, knowing him as I do, would be the first to acknowledge the contribution made by all you people down here at Palos de la Frontera. Now back to Don Carlos in Granada."

"Thanks, Don. We're now going to take you to Genoa, Italy, where Chris was born and raised, and speak to some of the folks in the home town who knew him as a boy. And we'll also talk to his parents. Will you come in, Don Diego?"

(Shot of gymnasium at Genoa High School.)

"Yes sir, Don Carlos, I'm standing here in the gym at Genoa High School and I want to tell you this is an exciting day here in Columbus's birthplace. Everybody in this town remembers Chris Columbus. Standing next to me is the principal of the school which Chris attended for a little while before he decided to take up a career as a sailor. Mr. Spinelli, what kind of a student was Chris?"

"He was a fine student and all the teachers liked him. Of course he never learned to read or write until he went to Portugal, but he was a good geography pupil and all of us here at Genoa High are mighty proud of him."

"Thanks, Mr. Spinelli. Now let's talk to Chris's best friend, Ponti Loren. Ponti, you were Chris's best friend in Genoa. What kind of a fellow was he really like?"

"Chris was always a serious fellow. I remember once when we were about eight years old and we were throwing some rocks at a Venetian, Chris said to me: 'You know, Ponti, the world is round.' I said: 'Forget it, Chris. Are you some kind of a nut? The world is flat; everybody knows that.' But he persisted. Chris was a stubborn guy, but he was loyal."

"Thanks, Ponti, and now let's have a word with Mr. and Mrs. Columbus, the proud parents. Mr. Columbus, as you know, is a wool weaver in Genoa. How do you feel about your son going into the unknown, Mr. Columbus?"

"You can't stop these young fools. I was hoping Chris would go in the wool-weaving business with me, but I guess he figures he's doing something important. Frankly, I couldn't care if the earth is flat or round. It don't put bread on my table."

"Thanks, Mr. Columbus. Now back to Don Carlos in Granada."

"Thanks, Don Diego. We have an announcement from the control tower."

"This is tower control. We have started the countdown."

"Well, folks, while we're waiting, let's talk to Queen Isabella.

"Queen Isabella, how much did this thing cost?"

"I sold all my jewels to finance it, so Columbus better be successful or I'll chop his head off. We've got to get to the Indies before the Portuguese."

"Thanks, Queen Isabella. Well, it's almost the moment we've all been waiting for. Let's go back to Don Alfredo at Palos, who is standing by the craft."

"Thanks, Don Carlos. The anchor has been lifted and in seconds the *Santa María* will be at sea. 10 . . . 9 . . . 8 . . . 7 . . . 6 . . . 5 . . . 4 . . . 3 . . . 2 . . . 1: there she blows! Good luck, Chris, and if you don't find a new route to the Indies, we're all praying that you'll be the first to discover America."

Everybody Is Doing It

EVERYBODY I talked to was impressed by Mrs. John F. Kennedy's television tour of the White House, and I believe Mrs. Kennedy has made a great contribution to the American home because she has made people conscious of their own surroundings and furniture.

Probably no one was more influenced by the program than my own sister who lives in Kew Gardens, Long Island. I went over to her apartment on the Sunday after Mrs. Kennedy showed the White House, and my sister was waiting at the door to give me a guided tour.

"Thank you for coming," she said. "I'd like to show you around because I feel that's the only way people can understand our heritage."

"Well, it's awfully kind of you to let us come here, Mrs. Jaffe. Where shall we begin?"

"I think we ought to start with the East Room," she said. "We call it the East Room because it overlooks the Eighth Avenue subway and Queens Boulevard—at least it did until someone built an apartment across from us and blocked the view. The East Room was originally intended as an audience room where we could meet our in-laws, our insurance agent, and our son's teacher when he got in trouble at school.

"But now it's gradually become associated with other events. Our large receptions are held here because, as you can see, this room can hold as many as twelve people at one time."

"Would you describe some of the furniture to me?" I asked her.

"I'd be delighted. That couch over there, the one with the stuffing coming out of it, is an early Franklin D. Roosevelt period piece donated to us by Aunt Molly, who said she was going to throw it out anyway. Aunt Molly used it all during the Depression and it has a great deal of historical interest.

"That lamp over there is a rare pre-Pearl Harbor Macy basement special. It was a wedding gift donated by Mr. and Mrs. Arthur Gordon, of Forest Hills, New York, and there are only 65,900 of them left in the United States."

"Is that the oldest thing in the house?" I asked her.

"No, the hot-water heater is the oldest thing in our house, but that's in another room."

We walked into what my sister calls the Blue Room, because this is the room in the house that depresses her the most.

"There are many things in this room that do have a historical interest," she said. "That bed there, for example, is an early Truman Gimbel's four-poster, which was donated to us by the Friendly Long Island Finance Company. It was given to us on the day that Mr. Truman had a fight with a Washington music critic over his daughter's voice, so naturally it has sentimental value. Actually, it's been taken away twice, but it has always turned up again after we made the payments."

"Those are lovely paintings on the wall," I said.

"Yes, they are," Mrs. Jaffe said. "This one here, which is a snow scene, was donated by Uncle Oscar, of Brooklyn, New York, who painted it himself and gave it to us as a present on the condition we would never sell it. There were a couple of numbers on the paintings that he forgot to fill in, but otherwise it's very decorative.

"I'd like to point out one more thing, and that is our President Monroe television set, which is probably the most valuable antique in the room. The television tube for the set was made by a famous glassblower who died somewhere around 1856. Every week we have someone come in to restore it. My husband believes if you have a piece of antique furniture you should never let it go."

"We're running out of time," I said. "Is there any other room you would like to show us?"

"There is the Red Room, where my thirteen-year-old son David holds his state receptions."

She led me toward it, but when she opened the door she slammed it closed immediately. "If I've told that damn kid once I've told him a million times to clean up his room."

"Well, are there any other rooms in the house we could visit?"

She looked at me funny. "What other rooms? That's all we got."

Destiny's Deckhand

EVERYBODY seems to be writing a book about President Kennedy's experiences as PT-boat commander in the South Pacific during World War II. Minute-by-minute accounts of his years at sea have been written by Robert J. Donovan, Richard Tregaskis, and many others. The literary rights of every Japanese and native who was within 300 miles of the place where Mr. Kennedy's PT-109 was rammed by a Japanese destroyer have been tied up by either *Life* or *The Saturday Evening Post*. Probably the only man who was in the South Pacific battle zone at the same time as President Kennedy and hasn't had his experiences published yet is Ichiro Kuichi.

He has been in New York the past several days putting the final touches on his book, called *Destiny's Deckhand—the*

Autobiography of a Seaman on the Japanese Destroyer that Missed Ramming PT-109.

I had lunch with Mr. Kuichi and Dick Lingeman. Mr. Lingeman bought the serialization rights to *Destiny's Deckhand* and has been acting as Mr. Kuichi's agent while the Japanese seaman is in New York.

He sketched in Mr. Kuichi's background for me.

Ichiro Kuichi was a rice polisher for the Koba Soba rice flour company in Japan. On the day of Pearl Harbor, after the Americans fired on the poor, helpless Japanese aircraft who were attacking them, Ichiro joined the Japanese Navy to avenge, as his Emperor put it, "this day of infamy."

His first assignment was as a suicide *kamikaze* pilot, but after he had completed ten missions his superiors decided he had an inadequate death wish, and he was kicked out of the Japanese Naval Air Force in disgrace and assigned as a mess boy on destiny's destroyer.

It was in this capacity that Mr. Kuichi played a role that was to change the course of history, not only in the United States but in the world.

Nobody knew it, but there were two Japanese destroyers coming down the strait that fateful night when John Kennedy was commanding the PT-109. One was Mr. Kuichi's and the other was the destroyer that actually rammed Mr. Kennedy. Mr. Kuichi's destroyer had first crack at ramming Mr. Kennedy's boat, but thanks to Mr. Kuichi it missed.

This is what happened, in Mr. Kuichi's own words:

"It very dark. I on bridge serving green tea to duty officer and helmsman. I very nervous because I know somewhere out there in dark is future President of United States in torpedo boat. I drop tea on duty officer's lap and he yells: 'You stupid fisherman.' In Japanese that sounds like 'hard rudder right.' Obedient helmsman swings wheel right and instead of ramming PT-109 with future President on board, we miss boat completely and sink PT-110 instead. All crew survived but nobody important on PT-110.

"Captain of my destroyer is very mad because after war

he wants to go into politics and he knows it would be very popular issue if he can say he ram President of United States in boat and give him bad back.

"But it too late, because other Jap destroyer with captain, who also wants to go into politics, sees PT-109, and he rams it. We hear cheers on other Jap destroyer because they know after war they can sell their story to *Saturday Evening Post* and *Herald Tribune* for millions of yen. Nobody talks to me on my destroyer because American magazines won't give a bag of rice for how we sunk PT-110."

Despite Mr. Kuichi's sad experience, he is still a big President Kennedy fan. He idolizes the President and even changed his wife's name from Machinko to Jackinto. He wanted to name his first daughter Caroline but didn't because he couldn't pronounce the *l*.

While in the United States he plans to autograph books (by any Japanese author, since the autographs all look alike) and he also hopes to meet the President and his family.

"President Kennedy very very nice to Jap sailors who sink him, so I think he should maybe be nice to Jap sailors who miss him altogether."

The Beautiful Spot

THE American magazine industry is going through a rough period, and more and more publications are appealing to special groups. There are magazines for bachelors, magazines for brides, magazines for hi-fis, and magazines for lowbrows.

Two friends of mine, Jerry Jonas, currently with *The New Yorker*, and Bud Trillin, of *Time* magazine, are trying to put out a new publication called *Beautiful Spot*, the magazine of parking, written and edited for people who have now or hope to have parking problems.

"You see, in New York," Mr. Jonas told me, "we have alternate parking. You have to change the parking place of your car from one side of the street to the other. You have to do it between 11 A.M. and 1 P.M. But most people sit in their cars from 9 A.M. on so they can get a good spot across the street. These people have nothing to read while they're waiting and that's where we hope *Beautiful Spot* will fill the vacuum."

"What kind of features will you have?" they asked me to ask them.

"You know *Playboy* has the 'Playmate of the Month,' which is a triple fold-out page—well, we're going to have the 'Beautiful Parking Spot of the Month.' It will be so bare it will make every driver's mouth water."

Mr. Jonas said: "We will also have a medical section aimed at doctors, discussing with them the problems of double parking in New York, or, as it is now called, Parkingsin's Disease.

"We're going to hit hard and pull no punches. We will have a feature exposing the UN iron-curtain diplomats for taking up good parking space that belongs to the free world."

"And," said Mr. Trillin, "we will have the largest news-gathering service of any parking magazine in the world. Of course, we'll pay space rates.

"We will have a theater critic whose job will be to report on flop shows. A flop show means a good parking situation."

Mr. Jonas said: "This will be a public-service publication. In each issue we will put in a perforated five-dollar bill which the reader can tear out and slip to a cop in case he is going to get a ticket. Other people will think the reader is giving the cop a subscription to the magazine."

Mr. Trillin continued: "We have signed up the best parking-guidance counselor in New York, who will write a monthly feature titled 'Can This Parking Spot Be Saved?'"

Both men told me that they had made a study and discovered parking was one of the most prevalent causes for divorce in New York City.

"Many wives can't work in New York because they have to stay home and move the car on alternate parking days. When a wife moves the car on Monday, presumably the spot she has moved it to is good until Wednesday. But some inconsiderate husbands want to use the car on Tuesday, even if it means losing the parking spot. Very few wives can take this because they feel that since they stay home only to find a good parking spot, their husbands should leave their damn hands off the car.

"If a husband does it more than once, the marriage always goes on the rocks."

"We believe," said Mr. Jonas fervently, "that parking is man's God-given right and that our forefathers, although they didn't mention parking in the Constitution as such, included it in the unwritten Bill of Rights. Where would we be if Paul Revere had pulled up in front of Sam Adams's house and had had to double park his horse?"

"Everyone is wondering what people will be doing when the work day gets shorter and people have more leisure time," Mr. Trillin said. "The answer is, They will use that leisure time to find a beautiful spot. One of our first features will be an article titled 'How I Parked My Car Illegally and Made $50,000 in My Spare Time.'"

Down on the Ant Farm

SOMEONE gave my son an ant farm as a present, and in order to explain it to him I had to find out about ants myself.

It seems that selling ant farms is a million-dollar business, and watching ants working is getting to be a very popular way of getting away from television. An ant farm even looks like a television set, except the show is live. The company which manufactures them supplies the sand and the glass, and then air mails 15 ants or 35 ants, depending on the size of the farm, to the customer. If he prefers to supply his own ants, they will send the customer a magnifying glass instead.

Mr. Frank Shain, who represents the ant-farm people in

New York and New Jersey, said that ants are becoming very popular pets, at least with children.

All they do is work and build things. They are easy to take care of and require a cent a year's worth of food. (There is no money to be made in the ant-food business.) If an ant dies while working, the other ants bury him, saving the owner a costly funeral bill.

The ant-breeding capital of the United States is Burbank, California, where all the red female worker ants come from. The company pays a penny an ant to any wild-ant hunters, but breeds most of the ants itself. For this purpose it has queen ants. The male ants don't have to work, but once they mate with the queen they die. Therefore only female ants are supplied as workers. The queen ants are not permitted to be sent through the mails across state lines, as this is a violation of the Mannt Act. Also, if Mr. Shain supplied queen ants, his customers wouldn't order new ants when the others passed away.

Mr. Shain said that there is no chance of an ant escaping from an ant farm, as they are all on the honor system. But if an ant did manage to escape, the other ants would go after her, because one less ant at an ant farm just means more work for the other ants.

But parents worry about fugitive ants, and one of the most frequent questions that Mr. Shain has to answer is "How are you going to keep them down on the farm after they've seen the dining room table?"

The worst time of year for selling ant farms, Mr. Shain said, is from May until September. The reason for this is that people see so many ants outdoors on picnics and the beach for free that they see no reason to pay to see them at home.

The thing about ants is that they stick together on their farms and won't tolerate outside ant colonies. At a recent toy fair some New Jersey black ants were placed by mistake in a farm consisting of Southern California red ants, and the New Jersey ants wiped out the Southern California colony. Southern California breeders immediately instituted a physi-

cal-fitness program for their ants so it would never happen
again.

One of the most exciting things about owning an ant farm
is trying to catch the ants sleeping. No matter what the time
of the day or night, ant-farm owners will usually find the
ants working, and after a while it starts to bug the people.
Apparently ants are so afraid that people won't think they're
working hard enough that they only grab brief naps when
no one is watching them.

One woman who owns a farm gets bored, so she waits
until they get the tunnels built and the bridges constructed,
and when they're pretty well set she takes the ant farm off
her wall, shakes it up, and makes the ants start all over again.

"Don't ants ever relax at all?" I asked Mr. Shain.

"Very rarely," he said; "they prefer to work."

"Well, what do they do for relaxation?"

"They watch people."

Dream Interview I

EVERYONE, no matter what his business, has a dream of glory.
Since I'm in the newspaper trade, my dream of glory is
getting an interview with someone like Nikita S. Khrushchev.

The dream always goes something like this:

KHRUSHCHEV: Mr. Buchwald, the reason I called you to
Moscow is that you're the only newspaperman I can trust.

MR. B: Thank you very much, sir. I have always been known
for my intergrity, if I must say so myself.

KHRUSHCHEV: I'm willing to grant you an interview, but first
I would like you to report our conversation to President
Kennedy. I feel that if he hears the words directly from you
he'll believe them, whereas he may doubt me if I go through
your American Ambassador here.

MR. B: There's always that chance, sir. I shall see President

Kennedy as soon as I get back, and won't print our interview until he is fully briefed on the situation.

KHRUSHCHEV: Good boy. I knew I could count on you.

MR. B: What would you like to say, sir?

KHRUSHCHEV: Well, I've been thinking it over and I've decided I've been wrong on a lot of issues. I guess it's my pigheaded peasant background.

MR. B: What issues are you referring to?

KHRUSHCHEV: This business about Berlin. I think the West has a point on West Berlin. The way I see it the whole trouble seems to be with East Germany. Our system hasn't been working there and they should have a chance to try another one. It was a mistake to communize East Germany in the first place. I think they should have a chance at their own government.

MR. B: Suppose they choose to go with West Germany?

KHRUSHCHEV: If that will make the East Germans happy, then it's no skin off my back.

MR. B: What about nuclear testing, sir?

KHRUSHCHEV: Now that I look back on it, I think it was a big mistake to resume nuclear testing. If I had to make the decision again I would have told my people: "If they want to test, let them test, but at least our consciences will be clear."

MR. B: But what about inspection to guarantee that there won't be any tests in the Soviet Union?

KHRUSHCHEV: They've got a right to ask for inspection. After all, why should any country take our word for it when we say we aren't going to test? I think mutual inspection would be a wonderful thing. I would welcome American inspection whether it would be done by flying over our country or be teams of U.S. scientists. The Soviet Union has nothing to hide.

MR. B: You're going too fast.

KHRUSHCHEV: I'm sorry. I didn't realize you didn't take shorthand.

MR. B: Sir, I would like to raise with you the question of Vietnam and Southeast Asia. The United States is worried that

Communist forces there are being supplied by the Soviet Union.

KHRUSHCHEV: I'll be frank with you. The idea occurred to us, but then we were worried about world opinion so we decided not to do anything there. We are very concerned about our world image and if we do anything that might anatagonize any of the existing governments, I say nuts to the revolution. It isn't worth it.

MR. B: What do you think of NATO?

KHRUSHCHEV: I think it's a fine organization and something the West should be proud of. I only wish our own Warsaw Pact nations were as well trained and prepared.

MR. B: What about Castro? How do you feel about him?

KHRUSHCHEV: At first I was very sympathetic with him, but now that I see what he's doing to Cuba, I consider him some sort of a nut.

MR. B: Mr. Khrushchev, how do you think we can get along with each other and have a true peace?

KHRUSHCHEV: I think the only way is for the Soviet Union to admit its mistakes and show the rest of the world we're ready to take our place in the community of nations again. For this reason I've urged Communist Parties all over the world to stop interfering in politics. I've recalled all our spies, and I've ordered our embassies abroad to stop wire-tapping other embassy telephones. If the Soviet Union has to resort to underhanded methods to get its information, I for one would rather not know what's going on.

MR. B: Well, thank you very much, sir, for the enlightening interview.

KHRUSHCHEV: Don't be silly, It was my pleasure. Would you like to stay for dinner?

MR. B: No, thank you. I think I better get his interview back to the President.

I shake hands and leave. The only trouble with my dream is that in it President Kennedy always refuses to see me.

Dream Interview II

I KEEP having these dreams of glory and they always seem to take the form of interviews with some great world figure. The last dream I had was with General de Gaulle.

DE GAULLE: Mon vieux, it's wonderful to meet you at long last. I don't agree with everything you write, but I certainly read you.

MR. B: Merci, Monsieur le Président.

DE GAULLE: Please, call me Charles. You know how I hate to stand on ceremony.

MR. B: Merci, Monsieur Charles. Cher ami, the people in France seem to be very happy that you managed to get a cease-fire in Algeria.

DE GAULLE: It was nothing. Anyone could have done it. I don't believe that one man can control any events. Things just happen, and in this case I was lucky.

MR. B: But everyone says if it hadn't been for you there would never have been a cease-fire.

DE GAULLE: People exaggerate. If anything, it was the French politicians of *all* the parties who helped me. Without them or Parliament I could never have accomplished anything. Frankly, I've always preferred to play a role in the background. I think it's a mistake for someone like myself to do anything without the will of the people.

MR. B: Some people, though, feel that you have too much power.

DE GAULLE: It is a justified criticism. I don't want any powers. I don't need any powers. The French people know what is good for them without me telling them. I believe if France ever hopes to become a great nation we must have a strong Parliament and a weak Executive. This is what I've been working for.

MR. B: I would like to move on to international affairs. How do you see France's position vis-à-vis the rest of the world?

DE GAULLE: France is just a small, insignificant country which must play no role in influencing international events. We first must put our trust in the United Nations, and then in such great world leaders as President Kennedy and Prime Minister Macmillan. They know much more about world events than I do. I feel we should go along with them on everything rather than risk breaking up the alliance. I would be a very selfish person indeed if I said France comes first.

MR. B: Then you are for complete European integration?

DE GAULLE: Exactly. Of course, this means a certain amount of concessions on France's part, but I see no reason why we shouldn't bow to the wishes of other countries if they feel we are wrong.

MR. B: Now, the question of the bomb.

DE GAULLE: Ah yes. In all honesty, I wouldn't mind having a nuclear bomb, but I don't see the real value of having one, particularly if it means testing in the atmosphere. As much as France would like to become a member of the nuclear club, I would much prefer using the money for social welfare and salary increases for the French worker.

MR. B: There is also the question of Monaco.

DE GAULLE: Alas, I must admit to making a mistake. Prince Rainier was right in kicking out my representative if he didn't agree with him. After all, Monaco is a sovereign nation, and what they do there should not be any concern of France's.

MR. B: Who would you like to succeed you as President?

DE GAULLE: There are many good men in France, any of whom could do the job. I don't believe any country should depend on one man alone. After all, France is not De Gaulle and De Gaulle is not France.

Antony and Cleopatra

RECENT events in Rome in regard to the making of *Cleopatra* have called for some serious rewriting of William Shakespeare's play *Antony and Cleopatra*.

Dramatis Personae: Cleopatra, Mark Antony, Octavius Fisher, Josephus Mankowitus, Caesar Skouras, Messengers, and Scribes.

Act One, Scene One. Outside Cleopatra's palace on the outskirts of Rome. Populace and Scribes at the gates. Cleopatra and Mark Antony pass by.

1ST ROMAN: Look where they come!
   Take but good note, and you shall see in him
   The triple pillar of the world transform'd
   Into a lover's lover: behold and see!

2ND ROMAN: The buckles on his breast reneges all temper
   And is become the bellows and the fan
   To cool a gypsy's lust.

A Palace Room. Enter Cleopatra, Mark Antony, Ladies-in-Waiting, Eunuchs.

CLEOPATRA: If it be love, indeed, tell me how much.

ANTONY: There's beggary in the love that can be reckoned.

CLEOPATRA: I'll set a bourn how far to be belov'd.

ANTONY: Let's not confound the time with conference harsh:
   There's not a minute of our lives should stretch
   Without some pleasure now.
   What sport tonight?

Octavius Fisher's Camp. Enter Scribes.

OCTAVIUS *speaks as they sit poised with pen:*
   I learn you take things ill which are not so,
   Or being, concern you not. As for my wife,
   I wish you had her spirit.

1ST SCRIBE: Mark Antony is every hour in Rome
   And so is Cleopatra. What say you?

2ND SCRIBE: The April's in her eyes: is it love's spring?

OCTAVIUS: You take from me a great part of myself.
   When it appears to you where this begins,
   Turn your displeasure that way; for our faults
   Can never be so equal as our love.

Enter Messenger.

MESSENGER: I come from Rome.

OCTAVIUS: O! From Italy!
Ram thou thy fruitful tidings in mine ears,
That long time have been barren.

MESSENGER: She denies nothing.

OCTAVIUS: Nothing?

MESSENGER: She did pocket your letter
With taunts, did gibe your missive out of audience.

OCTAVIUS (*to Scribes*): Oh misery on't the wise gods seal our
eyes;
Have I my pillow left unpress'd in Rome
And by a gem of women to be abused,
While I strut to my confusion?

3RD SCRIBE: Sir, sir, thou art so leaky
That we must leave thee to thy sinking, for
Thy dearest quit thee.

Exit Scribes. Exit Octavius.

*The battlefield of Cinecitta. Enter Josephus Mankowitus and
Caesar Skouras, Lackeys, Eunuchs, Bards.*

JOSEPHUS: Hail, Caesar! Let our best heads know
That tomorrow the last of many battles we mean to fight.
Within our files there are of those that serv'd Mark Antony
but late.

CAESAR: If you don't finish the battle by tomorrow I charge
thee all is lost.

JOSEPHUS: Hold! Do not yourself such wrong, who are in this
reliev'd but not betray'd.

CAESAR: Be it known that we, the greatest, are misthought
For things that others do; and when we fall
We answer others' merits in our name,
And are therefore to be pitied.
What news of Cleopatra and Antony?

JOSEPHUS: Upon her landing, Antony sent to her,
Invited her to supper. She replied
It should be better he became her guest;
Which she entreated. Our courteous Antony,
Whom ne'er the word of "No" woman heard speak,
Being barber'd ten times o'er, goes to the feast,

And, for his ordinary, pays his heart
For what his eyes eat only.

CAESAR: And what of Octavius?

JOSEPHUS: He has left Rome.

CAESAR: What said Cleopatra to him?

JOSEPHUS: She said: "You'll heat my blood no more, no more."

CAESAR: Ay. He comes too short of that great property
That now has gone to Antony.

JOSEPHUS: But that's not our affair. Let us make haste to the
rushes.

Nothing Like a Club

THE latest thing in flying is Group Discount Economy Fares.
It seems that if you're a member of any kind of club which
consists of twenty-five people or more you get a group discount which can save you as much as $200 a person on a
trip to Paris. To qualify for group travel your club must have
been in existence for six months before your departure date.
It doesn't make any difference what the club is all about.

This latest sales scheme to sell air-line tickets is bound to
make everyone even more club-conscious than they are now,
and many new clubs will be formed just for the sake of taking
advantage of the low fare.

But because of this there can also be complications. Let us
say some people in Hollis, New York, where I used to live,
form a club called the Public School 35 Alumni Association,
and they get twenty-five members to join. They meet faith-
fully every week for six months, and now the day before their
departure has arrived. Everyone is very excited, everyone, that
is, except Buzzy Dixon, who has just informed the others
that he has decided not to go.

A delegation is sent to Buzzy's house, where he's sitting in
the living room.

"Buzzy, what's happened? Why aren't you going?"

"I don't like Sheldon."

"For heaven's sakes! Nobody likes Sheldon, but that's no reason to cancel out now."

"Sheldon's always making fun of me at the meetings. In fact he always made fun of me even when I was in Public School 35."

"But, Buzzy, the whole idea of the club is to get an airfare reduction. We can't let personal feelings get involved."

"That's what you say. But it so happens I joined the club because I always wanted to belong to a club. I believe in this club. It could become something wonderful. But not with Sheldon in it."

"Don't you understand, Buzzy. If you don't go with us we can't go. You're the twenty-fifth member. We've worked and slaved for six months just for tomorrow. You can't let the rest of us down."

"That's the trouble with all of you. You think more about your trip than you do about the club. But the club means more to me than the trip. Sheldon knows that. That's why he hates me."

"Sheldon doesn't hate you."

"Well, he's always knocking down my ideas. I thought it would be nice if we had a clubhouse where we could meet, and maybe even a golf course, and we could have dinner dances every week and really be a club."

"Maybe we can, Buzzy, after we all come back from Europe. We could talk about it then."

"Sure we can talk about it, but Sheldon will veto it. He's always against everything I'm for."

"Buzzy, you shouldn't take that attitude. Sheldon likes you, he really does."

"No he doesn't. He even complained about the food when we held the meeting at my house. I can't stand seeing him once a week, so I see no reason to go on a trip with him. He'll spoil all my fun."

"But you don't have to travel with him. All you have to do

is take the same plane with him. Once you get to Paris you're
on your own."

"You mean we won't travel as a club?"

"No. We don't have to. We just have to be a club to get
the reduction."

"Well what good is that if you've got a club and you don't
want to see each other when you go abroad? What's the sense
of having a club? I thought we had some ideals. That's why
I joined. I thought we believed in the same things. But apparently I was wrong. I don't want to be on the same plane
with people who don't put the club first."

"You're right, Buzzy, absolutely right. The rest of us have
been selfish, thinking of ourselves instead of the club. Sheldon
is the one who has blinded us to the facts. I'll tell you what
we'll do. As soon as we get back we'll vote Sheldon out of
the club."

"He won't like it."

"Too bad for Sheldon. We have to think of the club, not of
any individual in it. The club is bigger than all of us."

"You can say that again."

"The club is bigger than all of us. Now will you come,
Buzzy?"

"Do you promise to build a clubhouse when we come back?"

"You bet we will, Buzzy."

"And can we have dinner dances every week, like other
clubs have?"

"And we'll have bingo nights and bridge nights and ladies'
nights and we'll make you the president, Buzzy, because
you're the one who has shown us what the club really means.
Now will you go?"

"Can I tell Sheldon what you said?"

"Yes, Buzzy, as soon as the plane takes off from the ground.
But you have to promise you won't tell him until then."

"Okay, I'll go. Boy, is Sheldon going to be mad."

Talk, Talk, Talk, Talk

I've been watching the disarmament talks now being held in Geneva with a great deal of interest. They seem to be taking on a pattern and they will probably be going on for a long time.

One has only to look into the future. The setting is the same but Ambassador Zorin of the Soviet Union has been replaced by Ambassador Groanyko and Ambassador Dean has been replaced by Ambassador Stone.

I take you to the 12,654th plenary session of the 17-nation disarmament conference in Geneva, in the year 1994.

Ambassador Stone is about to make a statement, but he sneezes instead.

AMBASSADOR GROANYKO: Your proposal is entirely unacceptable to the Soviet Socialist Republics.

STONE: But I didn't make a proposal, I just sneezed.

GROANYKO: I ask for a five-minute recess to confer with my staff.

(The recess is granted and Groanyko huddles with Soviet experts.)

GROANYKO: What should our response be?

SOVIET ADVISER: We could say *Gesundheit.*

GROANYKO: Yes, but how do we know the sneeze wasn't a trap to make us say *Gesundheit?*

2D SOVIET ADVISER: But if we don't say *Gesundheit,* and he really sneezed, it could be a big propaganda victory for the West.

GROANYKO: Should we ask time to get instructions from Moscow?

SOVIET ADVISER: No. It would look like we don't have authority to make decisions on our own.

GROANYKO: I think the best thing is to say *Gesundheit* with reservations. If it's a trap we can always renounce it.

(The session is called back to order.)

GROANYKO: Mr. Chairman, I wish to address a word to the Ambassador from the United States.

CHAIRMAN: Does the American Ambassador yield?

STONE: I do.

GROANYKO: *Gesundheit.*

STONE: I object to the Soviet proposal. They are not dealing in good faith and my government cannot accept their proposal.

GROANYKO: But all I said was *Gesundheit* in answer to your sneeze.

STONE: I request a five-minute recess to discuss this with my British colleagues.

(The recess is granted and Stone huddles with the British Ambassador.)

STONE: What do you make of it?

BRITISH AMBASSADOR: I don't like it.

STONE: Neither do I. I've sneezed before and they've never said *Gesundheit.*

BRITISH AMBASSADOR: If we accept it, and then he sneezes, we'll have to say *Gesundheit* to him.

STONE: If we give in on this, we may have to give in on other things.

BRITISH AMBASSADOR: At the same time it might be the opening we need.

STONE: I wish we knew. I could sneeze again and see what they do.

BRITISH AMBASSADOR: Or I could sneeze and see if they'll say it to me as well as to you.

STONE: Why do you think they spoke in German?

BRITISH AMBASSADOR: That's what I've been wondering. They've got something up their sleeves.

STONE: Suppose I say "thank you" on the provision that if they accept the rest of our proposals, we will accept their *Gesundheit.*

BRITISH AMBASSADOR: Good idea. It could be the first real indication of their intentions that we've had.

(The session is called back to order.)

STONE: I wish to thank the Soviet Ambassador for saying *Gesundheit.*

GROANYKO: I wish to object to the American Ambassador's statement and cannot see any significant change in the American warlike attitude toward these talks.

STONE: All I said was, Thank you for saying *Gesundheit.*

GROANYKO: I demand a two-hour recess to discuss this new proposal with my government, but I want to point out that unless something more concrete comes of these negotiations, they will have to be terminated.

CHAIRMAN: The meeting is adjourned until tomorrow morning at ten o'clock.

On Not Reading Books

EVERY once in a while I find myself at a dinner party where the question of books comes up. It usually starts when someone says: "Have you read *The Making of the President, 1960* by Theodore White?" Now if I've read the book I can feel very secure. But usually the books that come up for discussion are ones I haven't read, nor probably ever will.

So I have several choices. I can either lie and say I've read it and just hope the other person doesn't ask me any questions about it; I can say, as many people do, "No, but I understand the reviews are very good"; or I can say, which few people ever do, "No, I haven't read it."

It's very hard to admit you haven't read a book that somebody else has, and therefore everyone has developed his own method of handling book discussions.

One of the best ways of putting someone down is, if he or she says to you, "Have you read Theodore White's *The Making of the President, 1960?*" to reply something like this, "No, but have you read his earlier work *Fire in the Ashes?*" If this doesn't do it, you can always say: "I preferred his *Thunder out of China.*"

Occasionally the other party may have read these books also, so you will have to resort to a more spectacular response such as, "No, I didn't read the book, but his wife went to school with my wife."

That should more or less take care of your dinner partner. You can only return the ball like this if you're playing singles. If the match happens to take place in the parlor, with many players and spectators in attendance, you have to change your tactics.

You usually won't have trouble with Book-of-the-Month selections, because very few people want to admit that they're reading what everyone else is reading.

A friend of mine, when he is asked "Are you a member of the Book-of-the-Month Club?" always retorts: "No, I don't play golf."

People change the subject very fast in his presence.

Strangely enough, the safest books to bring up in mixed company are those written by well-known writers such as Faulkner, Joyce, Cozzens, Camus, Proust, or D. H. Lawrence. While everyone has heard of them, it's doubtful that anyone in the room has ever read anything by them, and you can even invent books you've read by them that no one else in the room wants to admit he hasn't enjoyed.

You can go even further with poets. Bring up the names of Auden, Frost, Pasternak, and Marianne Moore and watch everyone in the room run for cover.

Occasionally your opponent may throw a book by Arthur Koestler or Lionel Trilling at you, and you could find yourself treading water.

The only thing to do then is to challenge him by saying: "No, I haven't read it. Could I borrow it from you?"

This is a terribly vicious return and should be used only when you find yourself in a corner.

Scoring in this game is quite simple.

If someone brings up a book and you say you've read a review of it in *Time* magazine, you get a half point.

If you've read the book itself, you get two points.

If, after your opponent asks you about a book that you *have* read, you discover he *hasn't* read it, you get an extra three points.

If you've read a book that your opponent brings up and you didn't like it, you get six points.

Foreign books can provide the highest score for a nimble player. If someone asks you if you read Françoise Sagan's latest book and you can reply, "Yes, I read it in French," you're entitled to twelve points.

Each player keeps his own score, which is never revealed until he gets home that night, when he tells it to his wife.

Once he has proved himself, the winner can take his favorite Erle Stanley Gardner off the bed stand and pick up where he left off.

New-Wave Western

As PEOPLE who have followed the "Nouvelle Vague" motion pictures know, there is a new type of film, made by a new type of director, in which nothing happens. This lack of communication between the main characters is the essence of the film and reached its zenith in the French production *Last Year at Marienbad.*

I have always wondered what would happen if they used a New Wave director to make a Western.There is no problem finding a script for such a story. I happen to have written one myself. My picture is titled *Nothing Happens at Black Rock.*

My story opens, as most Westerns do, as the tall Stranger rides into town on a hot, dusty afternoon. The street is empty. As he passes the hotel the man whittling a piece of wood looks up and there is a certain recognition in his eyes. Then he goes back to whittling again.

The Stranger stops at the saloon and ties up his horse. This takes ten minutes. Once the horse is securely tied the Stranger walks into the bar, where the tables are crowded with

men playing cards. But the bar itself empties as he walks up
to it and says to the bartender:

"Gimme a shot."

"Double or single?" the bartender asks.

"What's the difference?"

"You save five cents if you have the double."

"I better have a single, and plenty of ice and water, please."

At this moment Blackie Jones, the town bully, steps up to
the bar.

"You a stranger here, Stranger?"

"Yup."

"You want to have a fight and wreck the saloon?"

"No reason to do that. I got no quarrel with you."

"Well, would you like to see who's the fastest on the draw?"
Blackie says.

"What for?"

Blackie thinks a minute. "You've got a point. Would you
care to play some poker?"

"Don't mind if I do."

They sit down at a table with five of Blackie's henchmen.
Blackie deals. The Stranger asks for two cards. Blackie takes
four.

They bet heavily. The Stranger calls and Blackie says: "I've
got five aces."

"There are only four aces in the deck," the Stranger says.

"You calling me a cheater?" Blackie asks.

"Yes, I am," the Stranger says.

"Okay, I'll deal over. No sense getting mad."

Two hours later both men have broken even, and decide
to call it quits.

As the Stranger gets up, he spies a beautiful dance-hall girl,
who beckons to him from her room on the second balcony
of the saloon.

"I wouldn't go up there if I were you," Blackie says.

"Why not?" the Stranger asks.

"No special reason," Blackie says.

The Stranger goes up to the girl's room. She's crying.

"You've got to help me. Blackie is holding me prisoner against my will, and if you don't help me escape I'll have to marry him."

"Well, you got to get married some time," the Stranger says.

"But you don't understand. Blackie is a bad man," she cries.

"A man that drinks the way he does, cheats at poker and steals girls and locks them up, can't be all bad."

Just then a cry of "Indians!" is heard in the street.

Two hundred fierce, painted Apaches come riding out of the hills waving their tomahawks and spears. They ride right through the main street and out again into the other hills.

"Gee," says one cowboy to another, "I wish I could ride like those Indians."

"I'd give anything to be an Indian," the other says. "I can't stand wearing these heavy cowboy clothes in this heat."

We cut back to the Stranger. The bed's pretty messed up and the girl is combing her hair.

"Well, see you around," the Stranger says, making a notch on his pistol.

"What about me?" the girl cries. "Blackie will kill me."

"That's life," the Stranger says as he climbs out the back window quietly, and leaves the girl crying on the bed.

THE END

This book was set in

Caledonia and Garamond types by

The Harry Sweetman Typesetting Corporation.

It was printed and bound at the press of

The World Publishing Company.

Design is by Larry Kamp.